molaíse of arran

a saint of the celtic church

by

Bill McLaughlin

ISBN-0-9535437-1-4

Copyright W.J.McLaughlin 1999

First published in Great Britain 1999 by W. J. McLaughlin
Taigh-an-Dara, Whiting Bay, Isle of Arran, KA27 8RE

Printed by Govan Litho Printing & Design Co-operative
Unit 10, Six Harmony Row
Glasgow
G51 3BA

ACKNOWLEDGEMENTS

I am indebted to Monsignor Roddie Macdonald for the gift of his translation of the Salamanca Manuscript. To Helen McSkimming, author of 'Dal Riata' for permission to quote from her work and for checking the accuracy of the genealogies. To my wife, Aileen for proof reading and helping to edit the text and to Dr Hugh McKerrell for helpful suggestions.

GLOSSARY NOTES

Where the Irish Language is mentioned by name, whether existing in Ireland or early Scotland, I have called it 'gaelic'. All later references to the language, in Scotland, have used the modern Scots word 'gaidhlig'. To differentiate between the two main characters called Aidan, I have referred to the grandfather of Molaise, Aedan mac Gabrain as 'Aedan' and to Saint Aidan who went from Iona to Lindisfarne as 'Aidan'. Words which are not usual in our language, today, are Cenél, meaning clan and Ulaid for Ulster. I have followed the convention of calling the Celtic Holy Men 'Saints'.

4

index

Introduction

Molaise was a Saint of the Celtic Church who lived for some of his life on the Holy Isle in Arran. It is the purpose of this book to deal with the life of Molaise in Scotland, not to the extent of ignoring completely his life in Ireland - which was the land of his birth and death - but to concentrate on his relationship with what is now Scotland and the Scottish Celtic Church and its Saints. To do this we have to say what we mean by 'Scotland' and 'Scottish' and to do this, in turn, requires us to describe the coming into being of the kingdom called Dal Riada for that is also the story of Molaise and Scotland.

CHAPTER 1

ᴅᴀl ʀíᴀᴅᴀ

At the end of the fourth century, Scotland, England, Ireland and Wales did not exist in the form we know them today. The Romans who defined these things until their departure in 410 AD referred to Britain as Albion, Ireland as Hibernia and the area north of Hadrian' s Wall as Caledonia. These names, however, described land masses rather than nations. The modern gaidhlig word Alba for Scotland is almost certainly a corruption of the original Albion for Britain. The Romans had a distinguished orator called Eumenius in the 3rd century AD who wrote in praise of the emperor Constantius Augustus and mentioned that the Britons were "accustomed to the Picti and Hiberni as enemies". The Picti were from north of Hadrian's Wall and the Hiberni from what is now Ireland, both areas outwith Roman authority. The "Britons" refer to the Brythonic people who inhabited most of the rest of the land mass at that time and who spoke a form of early Welsh. This is an important statement as it is the first historical reference to the Picti about whom so little is known but it suggests that they had existed for some time. The Hiberni had been mentioned much earlier in the reign of Agricola 80 to 85AD. Sadly, the old joke about whether Hadrian's Wall was built to keep the English in or the Scots out has no foundation in fact as neither of these peoples existed when the wall was built.

A significant change occurs between the 3rd and 4th centuries AD. In 360AD Ammianus Marcellinus said that "savage tribes of Scotti and Picti having broken the truce, were ravaging parts of Britain in the vicinity of the walls". We notice that the term Hiberni has given way to Scotti. This is confirmed in 396AD when Stilicho sent a legion to drive back the "Picti and Scotti". So Scotti had become the name for people from Ireland. History offers no guide as to why this name was chosen. What we do know, for certain, is how it came to be the name for our own country - Scotland - and that story is the founding, on these shores, of the kingdom of Dal Riada.

About 220 to 250AD there lived in Ulster one Cairpre Riata who was responsible for naming not only the Irish kingdom of Dal Riata but also, indirectly, the Scottish kingdom of the same name. His name, Riata, would first of all have been assumed by his tribe posthumously as was the custom. The prefix 'Dal' meant a portion or piece of land and was added to a tribal name when that tribe had become sufficiently important or strong to have an area named after them. The Dal Riata became, as we shall see, of enormous consequence in both countries. In Scotland, Argyll, took its name 'earr a ghaideal' - 'the boundary of the gaels' from their settlement there. It was a significant statement as it defined an area inhabited by a people who were different from the others in southwest Scotland - they were Celts, spoke gaelic and were Christian. In the 5th century this settlement became formalised when Fergus Mor, king of the Irish Dal Riata decided to move himself and the king-ship from Ireland to Scotland. Fergus Mor was a descendant of Cairpre Riata through nine generations and may have been one of the sons of Erc. We shall discuss this latter possibility shortly.

Saint Patrick had prophesied that Fergus Mor would "rule the Irish Dal Riata and Fortrenn forever". Fortrenn was the kingdom of the southern Picts nearest to Argyll. The Annals of Ulster are agreed that he came to Scotland bringing the kingship with him and that he came to exercise his authority over his subjects in Alba, thus indicating, clearly, that they were there before him.

This point is of great importance in analysing the widely credited theory that he had two brothers called Loarn and Oengus, that they were three of the six sons of Erc and that they came to Scotland at the same time with 150 followers. Bannerman doubts this and believes that the Senchus Fer n' Alban was edited by a subsequent author who simply uses the three names twice over when naming the six brothers and calls them Fergus Mor and Fergus Becc, Oengus Mor and Oengus Becc and Loarn Mor and Loarn Becc (Big Fergus, Wee Fergus, Big Angus, Wee Angus Big Loarn and Wee Loarn) to make up the numbers.

The tradition of the three sons of Erc has been shown to be a legendary contrivance which does not occur in the sources before the tenth century. It is, nonetheless, only two thirds legend because Fergus Mor mac Erc was real enough. His obituary was entered at the year 501AD in the annals of Tigernach.

'Fergus Mor mac Erc, with the people of Dalriada, held part of Britain; and there he died.'

Oengus and Loarn are to be most realistically recognised not as 'sons of Erc' but as the eponymous forebears of the Cenél nOengussa on Islay and the Cenél Loairn around Oban who have been convincingly identified by Professor Archie Duncan as 'ruling kindreds of an earlier migration of Dal Riata to Scotland' who acknowledged Fergus Mor as their over king in the last years of the fifth century.

As cenéla were named after Oengus and Loarn it would be difficult to argue why this should be if they were brothers of Fergus Mor and the senior one and king of Dal Riata was ignored. The descendants of Fergus Mor called themselves the Cenél n' Gabrain after Fergus' grandson and were for long the ruling family of Dal Riada. This, in turn, indicates that the Cenél n Oengusa and the Cenél Loairn pre- dated the arrival of Fergus Mor in Scotland as it was only after an ancestor's death that a Cenél was named after him.

The various dates entered in the earliest sources for the foundation of the Kingdom of Dal Riada in Scotland are confused almost beyond hope of precise resolution but they can be taken to date the arrival of Fergus Mor and his warriors in Kintyre in the last years of the fifth century. The year 498AD entered in the annals of Clonmacnois is as plausible as any other, and, taken with Tigernach's date of 501AD for Fergus' death would indicate that his reign was of brief duration, even by dark age standards. His son and successor Domangart outlived his father by just six years before the succession passed, in turn, to his sons Comgall and Gabran, for whom were named the Cenela Comgaill and Gabrain, the two royal clans of Dal Riada.

It was the Cenél Loairn, ranged along the most northerly border of Dal Riada, which took the brunt of the Pictish onslaught of 560AD. If the annalist's entry of 'the flight of the Scots before Brude Mac Maelchon, king of Picts refers to them as it surely does, then their territory, including Iona, must have been effectively lost by the time of Columba's arrival from Ireland in 563AD. It also means that Gabran was probably a casualty of the conflict. Gabran is acknowledged by the annals as 'ri Albain' - which translates as 'King of Alba' though it may mean 'King in Alba' - but his nephew and successor Conall mac Comgall, is described only as ri Dal Riada.

The succession of the kings of Dal Riata from from Fergus Mor to Aedan mac Gabrain is shown in the Genealogy of Molaise. The genealogy shows that Molaise was a direct descendant of Fergus Mor via his mother Gemma. Fergus is remembered, in Arran, by Suidhe Fheargas.

So the kingdom of Dal Riata was established in Argyll as far north as Ardnamurchan and in Arran, Bute, Islay, Mull, Iona and the inner Hebrides. The centre of the kingdom was at the great hill of Dunadd, near Crinan and, today, there can still be seen there the footprint carved in stone which showed the crowning place of the king. Similar footprints can be found at Dunaverty

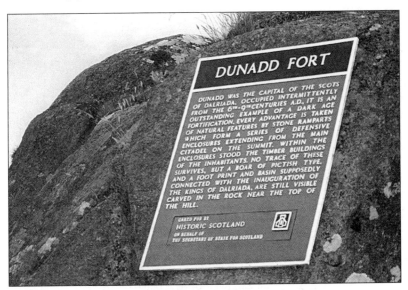

Inscription at Dunadd

and at Finlaggan on Islay. Dunadd was selected by Fergus Mor as his seat and succeeding kings of Dal Riata, including Molaise's grandfather Aedan mac Gabrain followed suit.

Dal Riada was the kingdom of the Scots in Alba and when, in 844 AD Kenneth MacAlpine united the Picts and Scots, he called the new kingdom Scotland. Accordingly, it is difficult to over emphasise the importance of Dal Riada as the cradle of our country. It gave Scotland its name, its language which it kept for almost 1500 years and its religion which it kept for 1200.

Helen McSkimming in her excellent and carefully researched book 'Dal Riata - from Erin to Alba' says "It is because the people of Dal Riata did not disappear into the mists of time like other migratory tribes from Erin that Scotland bears the name she does today. They were the Scotti of Roman times who had managed to survive and upon whom the later, Roman - taught and Roman thinking, descendants anchored the name for ever more. However, this was not the name they had for themselves. The idea of nationality or racial distinction was not the issue it is today, It is questionable that it was an issue at all. They were the descendants of Cairpre Riata and, perhaps at a push, they may have claimed to be of the Erainn."

The spelling of Dal Riata by the original Scotti and Dal Riada by the later Scots is simply a question of phonetics. Many gaidhlig speakers in Scotland today give a 'd' at that position in a word the value of a 't' to the ears of those used to English pronounciation and so later Scots spelled it Dal Riada. Little did Cairpre Riata believe in mid 3rd century Ulster that his descendants would give their name to and, indeed found, a new country.

The rock at Dunadd, the crowning place of the King,
showing the footprint carved into it and the bowl

CHAPTER 2

the celtic church

In discussing churches, it is necessary to remember the dictum that religion is inspired by God while churches are the work of men.
The distinction was made clear by Burns in the lines,

All hail religion made divine,
Pardon a muse as mean as mine,
Wi' her rough imperfect line,
As daurst tae name Thee.
Tae stigmatise fause freens o' thine
can ne'er defame Thee.

We have established that the Scotti brought their religion with them and so the Celtic Church came to a large area of Scotland. But what was the nature of the Celtic Church in Scotland and how did it differ from the Roman Church of its day? Both Churches believed themselves to be descended from the apostles, the Roman Church from Peter and the Celtic Church from John. Both were Christian and used the same sacraments. Both used Latin as their ecclesiastical language. Both venerated the apostles and the Celtic Church had a particular respect for the holy places of the early Church. Adamnan, whose 'Vitae Sancti Columbae' or "Life of Holy Columba" provides us with our major insight into the early Church in Scotland also wrote the 'Locis Sanctis', an account of those holy places given to him by Bishop Arculf who had visited them and subsequently spent time at Iona. There is a supposition in some histories that the Celtic Church did not have the same or, at least, a similar respect for Mary as did the Roman Church but this is demonstrably untrue. A poem written by Cu Chuimne 'to praise the Virgin Mary' in the time of Loingsech mac Oengusa - High King of Tara, and of Adamnan - both of whom died in 704AD begins:-

Cantemus in omni die
Concinentes varie
Conclamantes Deo dignum
Ymnum Sanctae Mariae.

11

Let us sing every day
Harmonising in tune
Together proclaiming to God
A hymn of the Virgin Mary.

The Celtic Church acknowledged Rome as the centre of Christianity but not, as we shall see, as its ultimate authority and it took until the 11th century for that situation to be altered finally. The three major differences between them were in nature, practice and organisation.

ηαταRε αηδ cαlταRε οf the celtíc chαRch

In common with other dynamic growths of the Christian Church, the Celtic Church took on many of the characteristics of the culture it was replacing. The Druids were worshippers of nature and the Celtic Church saw no good reason to attempt a total uprooting of these beliefs. Like Christ, they came not to destroy but to fulfil. Many first generation Celtic Christians had followed Druidic practices and had no difficulty in relating them to their new beliefs. Even many generations into Christianity this remained true and one in particular, the reverence for the sun, has a vestige of its practice in place today. There are many Christians who will rise at dawn on Easter Sunday to watch the sun come up and thus, follow the old belief that, if you do so, you will see the sun dance for joy for the risen Saviour. This reverence is the reason for the circle representing the sun which is inherent in the Celtic Cross, accentuating the importance of the sun when combined with the Cross of Christ. Although other interpretations exist as to the meaning of the circle - the unbroken ring of eternity, the halo - clearly, these all refer to Christ's resurrection symbolised by the sun rising on Easter Day. If the cross should be erected over a grave the symbolism is of the resurrection of the person beneath the stone. The Celtic Church attached huge significance to this location. One of the major reasons for the wandering of the 'peregrini' and for the whole practice of 'peregrinatio' was 'to seek the place of one's resurrection.' This explains why so many of the holy men of the early Church undertook journeys with no apparent point or preconceived destination. They believed that they would be guided to the place where their resurrection would occur. They were in no doubt that this was a very personal matter and could be influenced by no one other than themselves. This vital concept was inspired by the wanderings of Christ in the desert and the similar actions of the fathers of the Church. It is interesting to note that Columba in his 'rule' says that it is enough to withdraw to a place in the bounds of the monastery and to be solitary there in order to listen to the voice of God. This is, clearly, an indication by Columba that the choosing of the remotest places - as he himself had done - was less important than the achievement of solitude.

For this reason, Celtic Crosses were to be found in remote places but, sadly, almost all were moved by well meaning people to places of greater apparent safety and public awareness. This denuded the original site and left us with no reason to investigate it. The Cross which is, today, in Lamlash

Churchyard, is not a Celtic Cross and was brought from Holy Isle but may well have been erected, originally, at Cnoc na Croise - the hill of the cross.

Similarly, the stone slab with the effigy of Molios which is now built into the church wall at Shiskine was taken from the Clauchan cemetery where it covered what was perceived to be the grave of that saint. In recent times, Mr Andrew McCormack of Lamlash, while tending the Clauchan churchyard, uncovered a gravestone inscribed to show that it had replaced the one originally marking the grave of St Molios, so the site may still be identified today. A reference in a book entitled 'Pre 1855 Gravestone Inscriptions in Bute and Arran' runs, "Saint Malise died in 639 and is reputed to be buried at the centre of the walled cemetery. A mediaeval chapel was dedicated to him at Shiskine The site may have been occupied by the mission church built in 1708 and rebuilt in 1805. The Minister of Kilmory took services there every third week. A flat stone of the effigy of a priest holding a chalice and a shepherd's crook

The effigy of Molios which used to be on his grave
but now mounted on the wall of Shiskine Church

The stone now covering the grave of Molios

probably of the Cistercian Monks of Saddell and brought in the fourteenth century, was removed in 1889 and placed in the church wall". The grid reference is given as NR923304. Archaeologists believe that the original stone cannot have been in place in the cemetery for very long as its condition, in terms of weathering is not consistent with its having lain in the open since the 13th century during which Molios lived and, probably, died. This means that it was not fashioned until a later date or, alternatively, that it spent a significant part of its life protected from the elements. It is entirely possible that the monks of Saddell who were almost certainly responsible for its existence kept it in some sheltered spot. The stone, pictured opposite, is set into the wall of Shiskine Church. It is sad to read the inscription, on its replacement, shown above, that the original was "removed for preservation to the new Church on 9th July 1889". Unfortunately, its new site simply guarantees its continued erosion. We shall examine, later, the question as to whether Molios and Molaise can reasonably be believed to be one and the same person.

The ancients had seen the sun as the all powerful source of heat and light and had worshipped it accordingly. The Celtic Church simply taught that behind this was the power of God, that the sun had been created by God to provide heat and light and was quite happy that fire and sun should be reverenced. St Patrick replaced the fire on the Druids sacred hill of Tara rather than see it quenched. St Brigid, in her monastery at Kildare, maintained the sacred flame and it was watched over by 20 of the women of the place, day and night, in rotation, including Brigid herself who would leave her work in the fields or in the kitchen to attend the flame. That flame burned for 1000 years and was deeply rooted in the Celtic Church and the successor Roman Church. Only with the advent of Henry the Eighth and his destruction of the monasteries was it extinguished. Significantly, Molaise's name means 'flame' or 'light' and was a very popular name at that time as we shall see. The Celtic Cross was a development of the Druid standing stone with the sun at the apex but the sun was, now, shot through with the Cross of Christ, creation with redemption. The earth was important to the Celtic Church. Columbanus wrote "if you wish to understand the Creator you must, first, understand the creation." The Celtic Church understood the pagan beliefs about the oak groves and the sacred springs and wells. Columba instituted two of his monasteries at Durrow and Derry both names from the old Irish for an oak.

> The great cry of the people of Derry
> Has shattered my heart into quarters
> Derry of oaks we are leaving,
> Tearful with gloom and with sorrow,
> Leaving here broken hearted,
> To go to the land of the strangers.

Ian Findlay tells us that "Aedh gave him a place to build his church, the royal dun or hill fort at Derry, the name of which then was 'Daire Calgach' the 'oak wood of Calgach'".

Brigid's monastery was at Kildare, literally, "the Church of the oak."

While the Celts discontinued the Druid worship of trees, they nonetheless insisted on their symbolic value. They recalled that Christ died on a tree and that his resurrection brought life from the tree. John Scotus Eriguena portrayed the most sacred tree as being that in the Garden of Eden, the tree of life. It is interesting to note that the word 'Druid' comes from 'drus' meaning 'oak'. The Celtic Church built its places for people to meet and to worship from wood. The reverence too for springs and wells was continued, they being re- consecrated for Christian use. The great perception, then, was that the nearness and presence of God could be felt most immediately in nature.

It would be wrong to give the impression that there did not exist within the Roman Church those who held a similar view of creation. St Francis of Assisi would have fitted very well into the Celtic Church. He was derided by many in the established Churches for his primitive beliefs prompting Chesterton to write:-

When brother Francis pardoned brother flea,
He had much need of such great charity.
Because he is, despite his great goodwill,
Bitten by funny little creatures still.

Sadly, the more typical reaction of the Roman Church was that of St Boniface who deconsecrated all churches made of wood because of their perceived pagan connections and desecrated sacred wells and springs that had been Christianised. In this way, he dislodged the Christian faith from the earth itself and ensured that it would become immured within stone buildings. Happily, there is no evidence that his views were ever felt in Arran and, accordingly, no reason to believe that Molaise's Well on Holy Isle and Columba's well at Thunderguy ever suffered in this way.

The concept of pouring money and labour into great stone edifices and the belief that these somehow contributed to the faith and the worship of God was unknown to the Celts. We know that many of them visited Rome and had seen these buildings but they considered them to be peculiar to Rome and that they were a major factor in making pilgrimage worthwhile. The enshrining of the relics of the saints in great churches and basilicas was understood by them to be merely a continuation of tradition in a people who, throughout their history, had built temples to their gods. One recalls the lines from Macaulay's Lays of Ancient Rome;-

For how can man die better
Than facing fearful odds
For the ashes of his fathers
And the altars of his gods?

The Celts, however took a mildly cynical view of the value of visiting Rome and were clear that it was a pilgrimage of the heart. An old Irish poem runs;-

To go to Rome
Is much trouble, little profit;
The King of Heaven whom thou seekest there,
Unless thou bring Him with thee, thou wilt not find.

Findlay says "The fact was that a Roman saw achievement in terms of a stone monument whereas a Celt barely understood the idea of a monument at all." If we look at Iona today, there is nothing to show the nature of the church which was there in Columba's day. Bede remarked that when Colman and his clerics had left Lindisfarne sorrowing after the Synod of Whitby, the incoming Roman party found only so much by way of buildings as would maintain a seemly existence.

17

ɟeasts ɑnꝺ ɟestíʋɑls

The Celtic Church saw no reason to re-invent the wheel when it came to the Pagan festivals and the marking of the seasons of the year. It simply adapted them to its own requirements.

The Pagan year began with SAMHEIN which was celebrated on the first of November. This was the time when death was nearest and the land rested. It was also the the time when those beasts which were not expected to survive the winter were slaughtered and eaten. The bones were burnt on a "bone fire" and great feasting took place. Prayers were made for survival through the winter. The Celtic Church observed the feast of ALL SAINTS on the first of November.

IMBOLC was celebrated on the first of February. That is the time when days start to become a little longer and the light is with us for a further while. It became, in the Celtic Church, ST BRIGID'S DAY and, as we remember, it was she who maintained the sacred flame. It was celebrated as her festival of light.

BELTAIN was on the first of May for the Pagans. This was a time of celebration of the arrival of summer and hope. Today we celebrate, as did the Celts, MAY DAY but in this case it was the entire month rather than just one day which was Christianised.

LUGHNASA, named for the Druid god Lugh was the time of harvest and weddings and was celebrated on August the first. In the Christian Church, this became LAMMAS when the first of the wheat would be made into the bread for communion.

The Celtic Church carried on the observances of John in relation to the Sabbath. The apostles had maintained the old testament observance of the Sabbath on a Saturday. The Celts dedicated Sunday to God but continued to observe the Sabbath on a Saturday as a day of rest. The Irish Senchus Mor required every seventh day to be given to God in terms of "tithe and time". The rule of Columba provided that the special food allowance on Sunday should also be provided on a Saturday "because of the reverence that was paid to the Sabbath in the old testament. It differs from Sunday in work only". Gradually, by the eighth and ninth centuries, Romanising influence with its fear of following Jewish practices enforced Sunday rather than Saturday as the day of rest and Saturday became secularised.

In the area of celebration we notice that the Pagan poets were looked upon, by the Celtic Christians, as troublemakers. They frequently prophesied disaster for the Christians, they called down curses upon them and it was agreed about 585AD that they should be expelled. However, Columba at the convention of Drum Ceat in 590AD argued successfully against this.

He said "for you know that God Himself bought three fifties of psalms from King David. On that account, it is right for you to buy the poems of the poet and to keep the poets in Ireland. And as all the world is but a fable, it were well for you to buy the more enduring fable rather than the one which is less enduring" and he made this quatrain

If poets verses be but fables,
So be food and garments fables,
So is all the world a fable,
So is man of dust a fable.

He believed that they had a part to play in the advancement of all things Celtic if they could be tamed. As a result, Dallan Forgaill, a Druid poet, wrote the "Amhra Choluimchille" - a eulogy of the saint. Columba refused to allow it to be written while he was alive. Modern scholars date the very difficult language of this poem to about 600AD three years after his death. It is the oldest surviving poem in the Irish language.

The monks wore simple tunics with hooded cowls of undyed wool. Their form of tonsure was to shave the front of the head but to allow the hair to grow long at the back, like the Druids, rather than the 'crown of thorns' tonsure favoured by the Roman Church.

They understood three forms of martyrdom:-

White martyrdom by which they meant the separation of oneself from family and country, in other words a voluntary exile. In the case of the perigrini this implied going to a place from which one could not see even the shores of ones own country. It is this belief which is said to have caused Columba to journey as far as Iona. The ideal of the white martyrdom formalised the notion of the 'pilgrimage for Christ.'

Green martyrdom was that of the hermit who separated himself from all human company to attempt to commune, alone, with God. It was not always encouraged and many of the Celts believed it was only for the those of great character who had, previously, proved themselves capable of sustaining it.

Red martyrdom was the giving of ones life for Christ. The most famous example of this occurring among Molaise's contemporaries was the martyrdom of St Donan on Eigg with anything from fifty to one hundred and fifty companions depending on which version appeals. His story is told later.

None of the variations between the Celtic and Roman churches was in an an attempt to be different. It was simply that they had developed separately and had no reason to think that there was anything unorthodox in what they did. The form of tonsure, at least, was going to prove a serious problem when the Church of Rome began the attempt to force them to conform.

CHAPTER 5

Organisation of the celtic church

To understand the organisation of the Celtic Church it is convenient to start with the role of the bishop. In the Roman Church with its administrative system largely based on towns and cities, the bishop held great power. He was also the first step in the hierarchical pyramid. Although he was responsible to Rome he was very much the ultimate authority in his own see.

In the Celtic Church, the bishop was responsible only for ordinations and for evangelising. He lived, mainly, within the spiritual community of a monastery and was accountable to the abbot. He held no administrative responsibility. The Celtic Church went out of its way to ensure that the bishop did not get the opportunity of suffering from spiritual or corporal pride and accordingly they had only the same worldly possessions as anyone else in the monastery. When Columba was ordained priest, it is the tale of Angus the Culdee that Bishop Etchen was pointed out to him as a man ploughing a field. Columba wondered that such a man could be fit to confer Holy Orders but, "he tested him and was satisfied". So Etchen ordained Columba.

Saint Aidan, when he had been sent from Iona to Lindisfarne in 635AD was given, by the king, a fine horse upon which he proceeded to ride home. Happening on a beggar by the roadside, he immediately gave the horse to him. When the king heard about this he berated Aidan who replied "which is more important in the sight of God, the beggar or the horse?" The king instantly begged forgiveness.

The Venerable Bede, without whose history we would have little knowledge of the early Church, suffers from the defect of identifying ecclesiastical success with worldly conquest. The Celts never made that mistake. They did not attempt to use worldly power as an instrument of God's Kingdom.

A monastery consisted of a number of small buildings which could be increased as necessary. These would include the monks' cells which many historians believe to have been constructed from mud and wattle; the church itself was usually made of oak. Other buildings were the guest house, the refectory, scriptorium where the scriptures were copied, farm and work buildings and so on. When Columba's cell was excavated on Iona it was found to be on a mound with a commanding view of the Sound of Iona. He slept on bare rock with stone for his pillow. In practical terms, a monastery had also a maximum size which was never defined but was signalled by monks deciding that the sheer size and clutter of the place was coming between them and their worship of God. At this point a few of them would go off to found a new monastery in a quiet spot, later to be joined by others and so on.

The abbot was the soul-friend or anm chara of the community. One monk wrote "a person without a soul friend is like a person without a head". The abbot would be consulted if someone left to beome a hermit or pilgrim or evangelist or even to form a new community but the final decision was always that of the individual. Similarly, monasteries existed in respectful relationship with each other.

An Abbot was expected to be a pious and holy man. The story is told of Columba going off to pray on his own and being discovered with angels circling round his head. Adamnan's tripartite life of Columba includes a chapter entitled "The visit of the Holy Spirit which continued for three days and nights".

'When the Saint was living in the Island of Hinba, the grace of the Holy Ghost was communicated to him in matchless abundance and dwelt with him in a wonderful manner, so that for three whole days and nights, without either eating or drinking, he allowed no one to approach him, and remained confined in a house which was filled with a heavenly brightness. Yet, out of that house, through the chinks in the doors and keyholes, rays of surpassing brilliancy were seen to issue during the night. Certain spiritual songs also which had never been heard before, he was heard to sing. He came to see as he allowed in the presence of a very few afterwards, many secrets hidden from men since the beginning of the world fully revealed; certain obscure and very difficult parts of sacred scripture also were made quite plain, and clearer than the light to the eye of his pure heart. He grieved that his beloved disciple, Baithne, was not with him, because had he chanced to be beside him during these three days, he would have been able to explain from the lips of the blessed man mysteries regarding past and future ages, unknown to the rest of mankind, and to interpret also some passages of the sacred books. However Baithne was then detained by contrary winds in the Egean island (Eigg), and he was not, therefore, able to be present until those three days and nights of that glorious and indescribable visitation came to a close.'

There is an evident parallel here between Druidic practice and Adamnan's account. The Druid was the man of knowledge with his own unique access to the other world and the holy man in solitary retreat was in receipt of 'secrets hidden from men since the beginning of the world fully revealed.'

Druidic authority was based on secrecy. Nothing was committed to writing and the wisdom, lore and learning of the elect was passed orally to each new generation of initiates.

The second book of Adamnan's life begins with an account of Columba, like Jesus, turning water into wine. Water featured in a number of his miracles. A couple asked him to baptise their infant but there was no water nearby. Columba felt that God led him to a particular rock where he knelt in prayer, water gushed out and the baby was baptised.

The life of St Brendan says "and after the raising of dead men, the healing of lepers, the blind, the lame, the deaf and all kinds of sick folk.....after expelling demons and vices....after performing mighty works and miracles too numerous to mention, St Brendan drew near to the hour of his death."

Bede says of Saint Aidan "How great the merits of Aidan were, was made manifest by the all seeing judge with the testimony of miracles."

While these stories would seem to us to have at least an element of the mythical, they serve to indicate the regard in which the Abbot was held.

From all this, it is clear why they never felt the need of direction from Rome or elsewhere. While they acknowledged Rome as the centre of Christianity and understood that they held their beliefs in common with other Christian Churches, they believed that it was up to each individual to do his utmost for his own salvation according to the teachings handed down from the Apostles. This does not mean that they were isolationists. They were devoted believers in the value of the community whether spiritual or temporal and in the support which was so essential for each individual as he sought his salvation. Nor were the Abbots noted for their lack of severity. Examples of this severity can be found in Molaise himself, in Columba and in Fintan Munnu. Significantly, where a monastery was of both sexes, it was common to find it headed by an Abbess as, for example, Hilda at Whitby or Brigid at Kildare.

As this chapter is headed "Organisation of the Celtic Church" it is fair to concede that there was very little organisation involved as the Celts, quite simply, felt no need of it. They were perfectly capable of solving any questions as between themselves and we shall find examples of this later. They were not in the power or authority business, did not feel the need to become a world power, to dominate any of their fellow Christians or to produce dogma. They had a vivid existence untrammelled by the need for paternalistic organisation. They had all the common threads of a Christian Church in that they believed themselves to be part of one great universal Church; they believed a common doctrine as taught by Christ and the Apostles; they accepted the same bible and made exceptionally beautiful copies of it; accepted the same sacraments; this, they felt, was sufficient.

The Celtic Church had no need of money. The monasteries, as we have seen were utilitarian at best and built by the community. They worshipped in the beauty of nature rather than human architecture. Their bishops were looked down on by their continental colleagues as their clothing was so coarse and they had to accept hospitality along the way in order to make a journey. They went on foot rather than on horseback. They followed the example of Christ to the letter.

Any money which came their way was given to the poor or used to free slaves. When Augustine was sent by Pope Gregory the Great to deal with the Celtic Church he received many sums of money. He wrote to the Pope to ask how it should be dispensed. The Pope replied that it should be allocated a quarter to the bishops, a quarter to the clergy, a quarter to hospitality and only the remaining quarter to the poor. The Celts were horrified. One suspects that, at least part of their horror was because he felt he had to ask the question in the first place rather than follow the example of Christ.

CHAPTER 6

the spreao of
the celtic chuRch

The first recorded event of the Celtic Church was the arrival of Ninian at Whithorn in 397AD after spending his formative education with St Martin of Tours in Gaul.

It was from somewhere in the Galloway area and perhaps having been captured by pirates that St Patrick left for Ireland in 432AD where there was an existing Celtic Church.

Brigid, born in Ireland in 463AD foretold the birth of Columba; "a young scion will be born in the north and will become a great tree whose top will reach over Erin and Alban."

Columba went to Iona in 563AD and prophesied its demise and eventual, renaissance, in these words,

In Iona of my heart, Iona of my love,
Instead of the monks voice shall be the lowing of cows,
but ere the world shall come to an end,
Iona shall be as it was.

From Iona went Aidan to Lindisfarne in 635AD and from Lindisfarne went Cedd and Chadd in 653AD to evangelise Mercia and the Saxons.

While Ninian's is the first recorded foundation of the Celtic Church, Christianity had been brought to Britain by the Romans 43AD to 410AD.

However, this Roman Christianity proved to be fragile. It was brought by a conquering invader with an alien culture to a subject people. It was, clearly, confined to those parts only where the Romans held sway. Even there, it had no depths among the people and seems to have been confined to those who had commercial reason for dealing with the invaders. With the departure of the Romans in 410AD Britain was open to invasion by the Saxons who destroyed the churches and with them the structure of the religion. It is worth noting, in this connection, that the Norse invaders who sacked the Celtic monasteries on what appears to have been an approximate four year cycle left Celtic Christianity largely unaffected - they couldn't destroy the Church simply by destroying the monasteries. They could and did by slaughtering the monastics. The faith and the fabric existed independently of each other. In any event, the re-building of a Celtic monastery was simple and inexpensive. The spirituality of the Church appeared to make it safe against all predators; but then came Augustine.

CHAPTER 7

αugustíne

Augustine, as we have seen, was sent to Britain in 597AD by Pope Gregory the Great. Gregory was concerned at the fragmentation of the Christian Church and he sent emissaries to those areas which he hoped to bring under the control of Rome. The tale that Augustine brought Christianity to Britain is, of course, absurd. A timetable of events of its existence in pre-Augustinian Britain is as follows;-

In 178AD Lucius, a Christian convert built a church on what is now the site of St Peter's Cornhill, London.

In 190AD Tertullion wrote "Christianity in Britain has penetrated even the parts the Roman army cannot conquer"

In 210AD Origen wrote "The power of God our Saviour is with them in Britain".

In 303AD St Alban was martyred for hiding a Christian Priest.

In 313AD at the council of Arles three bishops attended from York, London and Colchester.

In 350AD Athanasius wrote about the purity of the British bishops.

In 400 AD St John Chrysostum wrote "there are many churches and altars in Britain".

Augustine and his eventual successor Laurentius were sent to bring back into the fold the British and specifically the Scots whose independence caused much disquiet in Rome. At the same time, he attempted to convert the Saxons.

In his dealings with the Celtic Church, he got off very much on the wrong foot. A meeting was arranged with the Celtic bishops and abbots. He received them sitting down, at once an insult and a statement of authority. To men who had been taught that humility and sincerity were two marks by which they might recognise the genuinely holy man, his actions were capable of only one interpretation and they immediately withdrew.

Augustine based himself and his party at Canterbury. Kent was, at that time, the richest and most powerful part of Britain and it was natural that a Roman cleric would select it. There his influence spread quickly. The King of Kent's queen was a Frankish princess and soon the men of Kent were paying, at least, lip service to the religion which had existed under the Empire. Outside of Kent, progress was slow. Paulinus, whom he had sent to be Bishop of York, was rejected by Pagan and Christian alike and was replaced by Columbans.

Augustine's claim to be head of all British Christians because he was appointed by the Pope was angrily rejected by the clergy and monks of Wales at a conference on the Severn. However Kent was a strong base. It was then, as now, prime agricultural land and was developed by the industrious Saxons and became rich and influential. Moreover, the Saxons seem to have followed their King's command and embraced Christianity. Eventually, the perceived barrier to his progress was the Celtic Church, those happy men who thought nothing of walking hundreds of miles to carry the message of the gospels.

Augustine's problem with the Celts was that he did not understand them. The hierarchical and authoritarian style of the Roman Church was foreign to them. Their method was always discussion leading to agreement and if agreement was not possible then agreeing to disagree. Their great leaders could meet and discuss contentious issues in a spirit of mutual respect and good fellowship and whether or not the question was resolved these qualities continued to exist between them. Unity was of paramount importance to them and they were always willing to give and take to preserve it. Nobody had previously told them "you must believe it because I say it, you must do it because I command it for I am appointed by the Pope". They were well aware of Christ's words to Peter "Thou art Peter and upon this rock I will build my Church and the gates of hell will not prevail against it and to thee I will give the keys of the Kingdom of heaven". They believed that this was a clear indication of Peter's holiness, the reason why he and his successors should be head of the Roman Church, a complete justification for listening to his words but, they did not see it as an exclusive statement. Other Apostles they believed to be equally holy and in particular, their own spiritual leader St John. At the Synod of Whitby, Colman makes this very point when defending his date of Easter;- "it is the same which St John the Evangelist, the disciple beloved of Our Lord, with all the churches over which he presided is recorded to have observed".

The Roman Church with its insistence on its own authority and its readiness to split Christianity by defining any opposition to its views as heretical or schismatic or by excommunicating those who disagreed with it caused them great sorrow. They identified it as an organisation whose example should not be followed. They also found it un-Christ-like in that He had never advocated the persecution of others for their views. The only form of agreement it was prepared to tolerate was total submission to its own views. We who live in an age when Rome is apologising for being wrong in its treatment of the Jews, for its persecution of Galileo and the three hundred years of the Inquisition can have a certain sympathy for those who were caught in an early example of this method of dealing.

CHAPTER 8

easter

Of all the questions which separated the Roman from other Christian Churches and, particularly, for our purposes, the Celtic Church, the date of Easter was the most vexed. The bible says that, on Maundy Thursday, the date of the last supper shared by Jesus and his apostles, and the day immediately preceding his death for many Christian Churches, "It was the feast of Passover". The Roman Church had expended considerable effort in distancing itself from all things Jewish and in defining the date of Easter to avoid all mention of the Passover. It was, however, in the minority of early Christian Churches in its assertions as to when the correct date would occur. The advent of Constantine the Great 274-337AD gave an opportunity to provide it with a date which might lead to some sort of agreement. Constantine, a convert to Christianity, decided that his main work, as Emperor, would be to unite his Empire and he believed that the first necessity was to permit only one religion so that, his people would be united in religion and to be united in religion meant that there would be no divisions within the Christian Church. He thought that if they were thus united, they would be more ready to unite politically. In doing so, he was taking on a serious burden. The Christian Churches of his day were widely dispersed and existed in small pockets or regions but had no unifying structure. Individual sects were left to their own beliefs and, although the vast majority of these beliefs were in common they had many differences, the date of Easter and the question of Arianism, the belief that God the Father pre-existed Christ, being the most serious. Accordingly, he had to devise a method of bringing them together if he were to have any chance of producing unanimity. His solution, as we know, was to convene the great Council of Nicea.

The problem in fixing a date for Easter was that it occurred during the Jewish Passover which is dated according to the phases of the moon in the Jewish Calendar and changes from year to year. This, thirteen month Calendar was also used by other nations. The Greeks used the Hesiod Calendar of 12 months of twenty nine and a half to thirty days giving 354 days a year. In only sixteen years its eleven day error would have resulted in reversing the summer and winter solstices.

The Romans used a solar calendar. They had settled on this when Julius Caesar had invaded Egypt in 48BC in pursuit of Pompey and had discovered the Egyptian Calendar. The Egyptians were very much more advanced in many scientific fields and the calculation of time was one of them. As a result, in 46 BC the Roman Calendar was re-arranged to give three hundred and sixty five and a quarter days divided into twelve months and re-named the Julian Calendar. The length of the months varied and July, named after Julius Caesar, was given thirty-one days in his honour. Later, when Augustus became Caesar, August was increased to the same figure and February reduced to twenty eight days.

So, there were two calendars to deal with but more complications were superimposed on an already difficult task. For the early Christians who were, after all, Jewish, Saturday, the Sabbath, was the Holy Day, the seventh and last day of the week, however others who believed that Christ was crucified on the sixth day of the Jewish week -a Friday- and rose on the first day of the next week-a Sunday, moved the Sabbath to Sunday and marked it by a special service featuring the Eucharist. Constantine confirmed Sunday as the Holy Day, made it the first day of the week and so, rejected Saturday as the Sabbath. But what was the date, as distinct from the day of the week, of Easter?

There were two great anomalies in defining the date of Easter. The first was the difficulty of reconciling a Lunar and a Solar calendar and the second was that the Apostles offered no date for Christ's death in any event. We have to remember, in this context, that time meant little to them; for example, none of St Paul's Epistles is dated. Most agreed that Christ rose on the first day of the Jewish week, a Sunday but which Sunday? Matthew, Mark and Luke suggest the first Sunday after the Passover feast in the Jewish month of Nisam while John indicates another date in the same month. A retrospective calculation was required but no one in the Christian Church possessed the astronomical knowledge to make one.

We have noted that Constantine required unanimity on all of this. He was less interested in searching for an ultimate religious truth than in defining, for political purposes, a date which could be enforced on the whole of Christendom

His decision was to have done with divisive religious issues once and for all and Nicea was convened in the Eastern part of the Empire much to the disgust and outrage of the Romans.

CHAPTER 9

the council of nicea

Today, there is a quiet Turkish village famous as a lakeside respite for Turks weary of chaotic Istanbul, some eighty kilometres away. It is known as Iznik. Seventeen hundred years ago it was a prosperous Hellenistic city known as Nicea, Greek for "victory". This name appealed to Constantine who styled himself "Constantinus Victorus". The sessions were held in a large Basilica converted into a church and in the audience chamber of an imperial palace.

Having convened a council in the east of the Empire it was hardly surprising that it was, mainly, eastern bishops who attended. The Christian Church had permeated few areas in the west. Sylvester the first, the aging bishop of Rome was too ill to attend but sent representatives. It is interesting to note that at that time all major bishops were entitled papa or pope meaning "father" much as the Celtic Church referred to "our father Columba" or "our father Aidan". The council lasted from the twentieth of May to a date in June 325AD. We have noted that few bishops from the west attended and whether this was because of the difficulties of travel, the snub implied in its being held outside their area or because the chief subject for discussion -the question of Arianism referred to above- was not their problem and held little interest for them is difficult to say. At any rate there were more than three hundred delegates. The part played by Constantine is defined differently by the distinguished historians who describe it.

John Julius Norwich in his magnificent "Byzantium" says the proceedings were "opened by Constantine in a garment which glittered as though radiant with light". He sat on a low chair of wrought gold. Norwich states that Constantine triumphed. Every major issue was settled as he wished. He had established a great confederacy of the eastern and western churches and his own supremacy over it.

David Ewing Duncan in his celebrated "The Calendar" says "The council opened in the late spring, probably on 20 May without Constantine. He came a month later .....arrived at Nicea on about 20 June 325 and was immediately handed a thick packet of papers detailing controversies large and small among the attendees.......Ordering the bishops to set aside their arguments, he took the packet of papers and dropped it into the flames of a brazier. As it burned he told his audience that they must use this council to establish a uniform doctrine they all would follow - an imperative that became the guiding force behind the

Roman Church for centuries to come and would profoundly affect all aspects of life". It did indeed become the guiding force behind the Church and the structure for the authority which Constantine required both for his Church and his empire which he saw as inseparable.

As for Easter, no documents exist from Nicea on the subject although the matter was decided there. By 325, most Christians agreed that it should be preceded by a fast and that the sacred day itself should have some relationship with the full moon that falls during the Jewish month of Nisan. Some sects held Easter always on a Sunday and others on the approximate date in Nisan that Christ rose from the dead, which changed according to the drift of the Jewish lunar calendar. By the third century a rising wave of anti-Semitism among non-Jewish adherents added to the confusion as Christians became biased against using dates which depended upon when Jewish priests determined the start of Nisan to be.

A third choice emerged: linking Christ's resurrection to the Julian Calendar and the solar year by using the Spring equinox as a fixed astronomic date to determine Easter and this was the one which was used. Unfortunately no one knew how to determine a formula for fixing a date for the Spring equinox as it required a precise knowledge of the movements of the sun, earth and moon. Time reckoners tried and failed to determine a true date for the Spring equinox and, accordingly, for Easter so most churches fixed on a date for the Vernal equinox of 21st March as being the easiest way out of the quandry. They could not know that the equinox is not fixed!

Nicea produced the arbitrary formula, that Easter falls on the first Sunday, following the first full moon, following the Spring equinox provided that it did not fall at the beginning of the Jewish Passover. Given their level of knowledge it was a sensible enough method. Also, given their unwillingness to follow a formula which involved any Jewish reference it was, perhaps, inevitable. In a letter addressed to all bishops and Church leaders who did not attend the council Constantine wrote "By the unanimous judgement of all, it has been decided that the most holy festival of Easter should be everywhere celebrated on the same day". Further on, in a letter charged with anti-Semitism, he continues "We ought not to have anything in common with the Jews for the Saviour has shown another way".

The Council's solution was imperfect on the following counts:-

1. It defined a moveable feast which was a confusing notion for many.
2. It was based on a fixed date for the spring equinox which is not, in fact, fixed, of 21st March.
3. It failed to account for the annual 11 minute drift in Caesar's calendar. This meant that in Caesar's day it was 25th March, by Nicea it was 22nd and Roger Bacon showed in 1267 that it fell on the 12th March, a nine day difference! (Roger Bacon Opus Maius, 1267 for and at the behest of Clement the fourth).

Eventually, the pronouncement of Constantine was a major factor in splitting the Church east and west, Hellenistic and Roman. Rome used, in spite of Nicea, 24th March for the Spring equinox while Alexandria continued to use 21st March. Augustine of Hippo noted in 387AD that the Egyptians celebrated Easter on 25th April, the Romans on 18th April and the Arian Churches of Gaul, the 21st.

Many of the differences arose, as we have noticed, from Nicea's decision to use a fixed date for an equinox which was not, in fact, fixed, although neither they nor Constantine would be aware of this. The Julian Calendar was flawed with its 11 minutes per year drift against true time giving a day every 128 years. By Nicea the date of the equinox was already 3 days out. Thus the dangers of Constantine's attempt at imposed unity!

Bede, in the 8th century, one of Rome's staunchest supporters was aware that the calendar was in error and that, accordingly, the method of calculating the date of Easter was inaccurate. He had constructed a sundial which he checked every day to keep track of the equinoxes. In 730 he proved that the equinox did not fall on 24th March as Rome insisted and showed further, that another equinox fell on 19th September - 182 days after the 21st March which made that date correct for the Spring equinox. In 731 he discovered that the Spring equinox did not fall on precisely the same line on his sundial as before.

So how well had Constantine dealt with the problem? To set his conclusions in context it is vital to notice that he had become disenchanted with Rome as the centre of his Empire. He had become convinced that its republican and pagan traditions had no place in his new Christian empire. It was growing more and more out of touch with the progressive thinking of the Hellenistic world. Roman academies and libraries were no match for those of Alexandria, Antioch and Pergamum. Strategically and tactically it was in danger from the Samations round the lower Danube, the Ostrogoths to the north of the Black Sea and, principally, the Persians whose Sassanian Empire stretched from the former Roman provinces of Armenia and Mesopotamia to the Hindu Kush. Rome had become a backwater. Accordingly, he moved his capital to Byzantium which was later re-named Constantinople.

In January 326AD he returned to Rome and repeated the celebration of Nicea among Romans who were deeply offended by his holding his major religious conference other than in Rome. His political astuteness prompted him to assuage their hurt by endowing the great Basilica of "S. Paolo fuori mura" "Saint Pauls without the walls" He had, earlier given to Pope Melchiades the old palace of the Laterani family which became "St John Lateran" and the palace of the Popes for a thousand years and still, today, the Cathedral Church of the City. His most important endowment of all was the Basilica which he commanded to be built above the traditional resting place of St Peter on the Vatican hill. He had helped to create the physical infrastructure which would sustain the Roman Church to the present day.

His political awareness is beyond question and yet, in his major task of uniting Christendom, he had recorded a signal failure. He had, however, established the Roman Church as the centre of Christendom especially as the eastern, Hellenistic and Alexandrine Churches had to one extent or another gone their own way after Nicea. We are, thus, able to see that originally the Roman Church implied the Church of the Roman Empire but after the fall of the empire in 410AD the Church remained and, from an ecclesiastical point of view, became an Empire in its own right, determined, eventually, to become universal as its subsequent name implied..

the synoᴅ of Whitby—664aᴅ

The whole question of Easter was one of enormous sensitivity to the Roman Church and though, today, it seems a small matter over which to declare war, there is evidence that that is precisely what Rome was prepared to do to avoid any contagion with Judaism. As early as the second century Polycarp, who was a great friend of John went to Rome to attempt to resolve the question. It was, at that time agreed, that these churches should continue to follow the example of John in fasting on the anniversary of the death of Christ even if this date fell on a Sunday. In 190AD Ireneus went to Rome to discuss the matter with Pope Victor who was about to excommunicate all those who followed John. Again, union was maintained. In 325AD the Council of Nicaea defined the calculation as described above. Pope Honorius wrote to the Celtic Churches in 630AD asking whether they "in the farthest reaches of the earth were wiser than all the ancient and modern churches of Christ". The question assumed what it had to prove, the ancient churches having been anything but in agreement on the issue as we have seen. His letter had some effect, however and in 632AD Cummein, Abbot of Durrow wrote to Abbot Seguine of Iona to ask whether he deemed it right to say "Jerusalem errs, Antioch errs, Alexandria errs, the whole world errs, only the Scots and the Britons know what is right".

We have to assume that the Abbot of Durrow was unaware that Alexandria, among a host of others, did not celebrate Easter on the same day as Rome. The southern Irish accepted the Roman dating. In 640AD the Northern Irish Church wrote to the Pope saying they could not follow their Southern brethren and also that they had difficulty in understanding why it was so important to him to make them do so. Sadly, Honorius had died and the reply came from the Arch-Priest Hilarius accusing them of trying to revive the ancient heresy "rejecting with a cloudy darkness our Easter, in which Christ was sacrificed and striving to celebrate it on the fourteenth moon with the Jews". This was a fine piece of ecclesiastical double think as the Celtic Easter coincided with the Jewish Passover only when the fourteenth moon fell on a Sunday and that it was biblically accurate which Rome was not.. Hilarius, incidentally, omitted to inform Honorius' successor of this salient fact and so, ensured that the matter would proceed under a false belief. He did, however, concede by this statement, the true reason for the Roman Church changing the original way of calculating Easter - it smacked of Judaism.

Eventually, Rome was going to ensure that the matter would be resolved, and, to some extent at least, this was done at the Synod of Whitby in 664AD. The reason for the calling of the Synod is as follows. King Oswiu of Northumberland was baptised in the Celtic Church but his wife, Eanfled, was a Kentish princess and brought up in the Roman Church. In fact, her chaplain was called Romanus. They celebrated Easter at different times although the difference in the calendar could often be as little as one day with the result that the King and his court were feasting in celebration of Easter while the Queen and her retinue were fasting for Palm Sunday. The queen had the support of their son Alchfrid who had been brought up in the Roman tradition and instructed in its practices by Wilfrid of Ripon. Wilfrid had been educated at Lindisfarne but had visited Rome and had become an adherent of its views. Oswiu decided to resolve matters and called a synod at Whitby, a community of monks and nuns whose Abbess was Hilda, a staunch supporter of the Columban tradition. The chief protagonists were Colman, Abbot of Lindisfarne for the Celtic Church and Wilfrid for the Roman. The interpreter was Cedd also educated at Lindisfarne and of the Celtic persuasion.

The agenda for discussion included the date of Easter, the style of the tonsure and whether a person being baptised should be immersed once or three times. The latter two points are barely mentioned in any account of the proceedings.

In Oswiu's opening statement, his own position was made clear. He had been persuaded by his wife, son and others and was simply arranging to formalise matters. He said that those who serve one God should observe the same rule of life as "they all expected the same kingdom in heaven". Clearly, he did not expect Wilfrid to accept the view of the Celtic Church and the die, effectively, was cast. He then invited Colman to justify his position. Colman replied "the Easter I keep is received from my elders who sent me bishop hither. All our forefathers, men beloved of God are known to have kept it thus and that the same may not seem contemptible or worthy to be rejected, it is the same which John the evangelist, the disciple beloved of Our Lord with all the churches over which he presided, is recorded to have observed".

Wilfrid replied, "The Easter which we observe we saw celebrated by all at Rome where the blessed disciples Peter and Paul lived, taught, suffered and were buried". He then described how, on his pilgrimages through France and Italy he "saw the same thing done and that he found the same thing practised in Greece, Africa, Egypt and Asia and in all the world where the Church of Christ is spread abroad". In this last statement he used what is most kindly described as poetic licence - he had never been further than Rome. Additionally, in France/ Gaul the feast was, for the most part celebrated on a day other than that used by Rome! Against an opponent of Columba's mettle he would have found himself skewered for his pains. Coleman, however, was a gentle cleric and allowed the point to pass. Wilfrid, then conceding that the early Church had indeed celebrated Easter as Colman said, asserted that the early Church laboured under Judaistic practices for fear of offending the Jews. Again, an abler opponent would have seized upon this admission that those whom Wilfrid represented had changed the original and accepted practices of the Church merely to distance themselves from Jewish practices and not for good theological reasons. He would also have been able to point out that, at Nicea, it was the diktat of Constantine, which had over-ridden theological considerations and replaced them with the need for uniformity.

Wilfrid then said that what Peter had laid down, "All successors of St John in Asia since his death, all the churches throughout the world have since followed. You agree neither with John nor with Peter nor with the law nor with the Gospel in the celebration of the greatest festival". This statement, again, contained elements which were simply untrue. Peter, himself Jewish, had followed the Jewish timing and he pre-dated the anti semitic movement which had caused the unsafe method to be employed. John's immediate successors had not followed the Roman date - we have seen that in the second century, Polycarp had gone to Rome to attempt to gain agreement on the matter and that, in 190AD Ireneus went to Rome to prevent Victor, bishop of Rome, from excommunicating those who held to the old date. As for his phrase "nor with the Gospel". The Celtic Church followed the Gospel exactly in adhering, like John, to the Sunday following Passover.

Colman replied "Is it to be believed that our most reverend Father Columba and his successors, men beloved by God and who kept Easter in the same manner thought or acted contrary to divine writings? Whereas there were many among them whose sanctity is testified by heavenly signs and the working of miracles, whose life, customs and disciplines I never cease to follow nor questioning their being saints in heaven". This was a most difficult point for Wilfrid to answer. Rome was not accustomed to sanctify members of the Celtic Church whom it saw as being in political opposition to it and, therefore, he knew that simply stating a list of those whom Rome had sanctified and who accepted the Roman date would cut no ice with his opponents.

Accordingly, he then made what to any follower of Columba was the unforgiveable statement. "Concerning your Father Columba and his followers, whose sanctity you say you imitate and whose rules and precepts you observe and which have been confirmed by signs from heaven, I may answer that when many on the day of judgement shall say to the Lord that in his name they prophesied and cast out devils and wrought many wonders He will reply that 'He never knew them'".

This was a contemptible and disgraceful statement for one man of God to make to another. No spiritual humility here but a dreadful arrogance. A Roman statement born of the belief that it alone knew the word of God and could predict His future interpretation of human actions and was prepared to state these in anticipation. Immediately, he sensed that he had gone too far and said "Far be it from me that I say so of your fathers for it is much more just to believe what is good than what is evil of persons whom one does not know. Wherefore I do not deny these to have been God's servants (having just done so) and beloved by Him, whom with rustic simplicity but pious intentions have

34

themselves loved Him". It is a maladroit apology and, again, had he been dealing with Columba he would have paid a high price.

Wilfrid then made his final statement and, addressing Coleman directly said "For although your fathers were pious men, can you imagine that they, a few men in a far corner of a remote island are preferable to the Universal Church of Christ throughout the world. And even if your Columba or, if I may say so, ours also; if he was the servant of Christ, even if he was a saint who could perform miracles, can he take precedence over the most blessed prince of the apostles to whom Our Lord said "Thou art Peter and upon this rock I will build my Church and the gates of hell shall not prevail against it and I will give Thee the keys of the kingdom of Heaven."

When Wilfrid had finished the king asked Colman if it was true that the Lord had said these words to Peter. When Colman affirmed that it was, the king asked if the same had been said to Colum Cille.

Colman said simply "No". With this the King indicated that he would not contradict Peter who held the keys to the kingdom of heaven lest, when he himself should arrive there "he who holds the keys has turned away". The substantial point that Peter had not defined a date for Easter beyond the Passover, was not mentioned.

In all of this, Colman and Wilfrid were unevenly matched and we may take this view independent of any objective assessment of the date of Easter. Colman, true to his tradition, a pious and holy man, ever willing to listen to another's point of view and never even considering the possibility of personal attack on his opponent is faced by Wilfrid. Colman is there to defend his traditions. At no stage does he attack Rome. Wilfrid, the skilled debater is there to use fair means or foul to attain his objective including, as the modern phrase has it, being economical with the truth. Wilfrid is learned and, although educated at Lindisfarne has acquired the qualities of the Roman Church leader. He is dogmatic, authoritarian and will brook no argument. He attacks Colman and his tradition in immoderate language, judging, correctly, that a hectoring style will unsettle an opponent who is unused to this style of debate. It is interesting to note that, as a reward for his efforts, he became bishop of Northumbria but in 677AD was driven from his see by the very queen whose cause he had championed at Whitby. Sic transit gloria mundi! Perhaps even more apposite would be "put not your trust in princes" or queens!

At the beginning of this description of Whitby it was noted that, to a large extent, the matter was resolved. To the same extent it must be said that the decision of Oswiu was limited. Its immediate effect was felt only in Northumbria and specifically at Lindisfarne whence Colman withdrew and was replaced by Tuda, an Englishman, as bishop and, as abbot, by Eata. Colman and his supporters, including thirty English monks returned to Iona and subsequently to Ireland. We note that the verdict of Whitby was accepted by the Irish in 696AD, by the Scots in 716AD, and by the Welsh in 755AD, respectively 32, 52, and 91 years later. However, although limited in its immediate effect, it determined that, in the fullness of time, the Celtic Church would fall into line with Rome. Both sides seem to have acknowledged that Whitby would be definitive. Although, today, we see it as having resolved the Easter question, and, two minor matters and although these three matters need not necessarily determine the fate of churches, nevertheless it did so. The ultimate authority which Canterbury and Rome had sought they now possessed and used it ruthlessly.

In 810AD the Irish monks who who had continued to work in the south and west of England were forbidden to preach. By the early ninth century, on the continent, individual Celtic communities were being brought into line with Rome. In 817AD, Boniface imposed uniformity on churches with Celtic foundations. It was only in the twelfth century, in Ireland, that Malachy of Armagh imposed a uniform Roman liturgy and the Papal Legate, the bishop of Limerick required that all previous usages "give place to the one, Catholic and Roman Office." The Celtic Church continued to exist, as a recognisable entity for almost 500 years after Whitby.

So what is our judgement on the viability of the Celtic Church? Would the lack of organisation and accent on simple piety rather than political and religious awareness and the necessity for building corporal strength have caused the Church to founder as the historian Greene, suggests? Perhaps, but historians who re-invent themselves as prophets are of limited credibility. Greene argues that "England was saved by the victory of Rome" a view in which he has the support of the Venerable Bede. Had the Celtic Church won at Whitby, ecclesiastical history would have been a story of "tribal quarrels and controversies". "The clergy contributing no element save that of disorder to the state". He fails to notice that a continuance of the "simple piety" and the resultant saving of the clergy from worldliness as they were saved in the Celtic Church would have removed one reason for the Reformation in Britain. Also that the concentration of worldly wealth in the Church and its monasteries would have been prevented by a Church which saw money as being for the relief of poverty and thus a second reason for the Reformation would have ceased to exist. Is it possible that a Celtic Church with its continued responsiveness to the spiritual, its firm rooting among the people where it had an inspirational effect and its strong sense of community would have changed the ecclesiastical history of Britain? It would, but exactly how, we will never know, Suffice it to concede the point that it is difficult to imagine it contending with today's urban existence and materialistic outlook, although, in its heyday, it had contended successfully with both but on a much smaller scale.

CHAPTER 11

molaíse

Molaise, as our genealogy shows, had royal blood on both sides of his family. His mother was Gemma, daughter of Aedan mac Gabrain who had been created King of Dal Riada by Columba, and his father was Cairell, King of the Dal Fiatach and of Ulaid (Ulster) and Man. He was an important figure in the Celtic church, a founder of monasteries, who was at the centre of the great debate on the date of Easter and, when he died at Leighlin on 18th April 639AD was given one of the three greatest funerals seen in Ireland up to that time. In Ireland he was known as Laisren and in Scotland as Molaise. The root of his name is the same in both countries - Las meaning light or flame. He was born in Ireland to Cairell, an Irish king and Gemma a princess of the Scottish Dal Riada. She is described as Monadh's Lady Gem. Monadh was an area containing much of the West Highlands and Inner Hebrides and was quite probably an older name for Dal Riada.

Blessed Molaise, flame of fire,
Singing with his comely choir,
Rath-Gille Abbot, king of flame,
Son of Monadh's Lady Gem.

His oldest brother or, possibly, half brother Baetan was, for ten years, 572 - 582AD king of all Ulaid, Man and, perhaps Skye. Some Irish sources describe him as King of Ireland and Scotland (Ri Eren ocus Alban). The Kingship was offered to Molaise but he refused it and "retired to a certain island of the sea between Britain and Alba" which was, of course Arran or, more precisely, the Holy Isle and there, his sanctity marked by many miracles, he won the veneration of his people. The Salamanca Manuscript tells us that, after his birth in Ireland, Gemma "took him to her native land". Almost certainly, she returned with her father Aedan who had fled to Ireland after the defeat of his father Gabran in battle. They stayed, eventually, at Dunadd near Crinan which Aedan made his fortress after he was consecrated king by Columba.

Regarding his birth, the Salamanca Manuscript says "Signs when he was born foretold his holiness. The midwife, unable to bear children, took the child to her bosom; he made the sign of the cross and she became fertile. A blind man named Senachus had his sight restored after bathing his face in the baptismal water". "After this his mother returned to the land of her birth with the child where he stayed for seven years and did many miracles. There, to the astonishment of many witnesses, he saved his nurse from death when a snake had bitten her. When he made the sign of the cross on her wounded hand the poisonous swelling disappeared".

The "seven years" mentioned above is of interest to us in attempting to fix when he was in Arran and for how long. The most learned of our historians can shed no light on this but we may attempt a timescale as follows. We know he was born between 566 and 573AD and that Aedan was consecrated King by Columba in 574. If we are not reading the Salamanca Manuscript too literally and he returned with Gemma soon after his birth, then 573AD is the likelier date. It also makes sense that Aedan, Gemma and Molaise returned together in 574AD. If he remained in Dal Riada for seven years then he returned to Ireland in 581AD to be educated by Fintan Munnu at the age of eight. How long his education lasted, we cannot say but we know that he was asked by his people, the Dal Fiatach, to become their King. This would only have occurred when he was at an age to do so which supports the notion that he was a late teenager or young man when he returned to Dal Riada and Arran.

We are helped in our quest to assess his age when he was in Arran and also to calculate how long he stayed here by a vital piece of information. That is that he was ordained priest by Pope Gregory the Great whose reign we know to have been from 590 to 604. Accordingly, he was aged 31, assuming that the ordination happened in the last year of Gregory's reign and, somewhere between 17 and 31 given Gregory's 14 year term. As has been mentioned above, it is unlikely that he came to Arran much before the age of 16 or 17 and so, a 10 to 12 year stay seems a reasonable estimate. Later in his life, he was consecrated bishop by Honorius the first whose reign was from 625 to 638 meaning that he was not made a bishop before the age of 52 which was relatively old for those days and, he may even have been as old as 65.

Some of the events during his time with "Holy Munnu" indicate the high reputation he was acquiring. The Salamanca Manuscript - hereinafter referred to as the Manuscript- tells us "Having learned from his (Munnu's) wisdom and affected by his example he performed extraordinary miracles. One day while they were milling and there was an insufficient flow of water available, on his master's instructions, he went out and dug up a sod and there was an abundant flow of water for milling". Again, "when they knew, in advance of the arrival of pirates, the brethren were in the chapel begging God to keep them safe from the attacks of their enemies. When night was replaced by dawn they saw the robbers in the fields which surrounded the monastery. But as he prayed with the others the robbers retreated as though they were being attacked, abandoned their boat and fled like madmen to their ships".

Again, "At another time when he took some travellers under his care some pirates arrived who stripped them of all that they had. God took vengeance upon them and, after they had divided the spoils, they fell to fighting among themselves and they killed one another. Those who were with the holy man rejoiced and praised God in His saint and they arrived at their destination with the pirates loot as well as their own possessions".

At this stage, it is worth recording the detail of his grandfather Aedan's ordination as king by Columba as it is at once part of the genealogy of Molaise and shows the worldly importance to which he might have fallen heir had he so wished.

According to Cuimine, a later abbot of Iona, "at another time the holy man (Columba) while staying at the Island of Hynba, one night while in an ecstasy of mind he saw an angel of the Lord sent unto him who held in his hand the glass book of the ordination of kings. This book he received from the hand of the angel and began to read. Refusing to ordain Aedan as directed, for he loved his brother Iogenan more, the angel suddenly stretched forth his hand and struck the saint with a whip, the mark of which remained on his side all the days of his life. He also addressed to him this word. 'Know for certain that I am sent from God in order that thou mayest ordain Aedan King, which, if thou wilt not do, I will smite thee again'. The angel giving him the same things in charge for three successive nights, the Saint sailed over to the Island of Iona and Aedan coming thither he ordained him as King".

As we have now mentioned it twice in connection with visions of Columba it seems appropriate here to include a short note about this island of Hinba or Hynba. It may have had a monastery built by Columba in the very first days of his coming to Scotland. Adamnan says, "The venerable man sent Ernan, his uncle, an aged priest to preside over the monastery he had founded many years before in Hinba Island."

Nineteenth century historians place Hinba among the Garvellach Islands which lie to the southeast of Mull. This view was taken because of the existence on the most southerly of these islands of little drystone-built beehive cells. Professor W.J.Watson in his great work on Celtic place names examined Adamnan's references to Hinba in great detail. He noticed that Adamnan mentioned a 'holy man who came from Ireland and spent the rest of his life in the island of Hinba and led the life of the anchorite for twelve years more in the hermitage of Muirbolc-mar.'

Muirbolc-mar 'the big bag of the sea' would indicate an unusually large bag shaped bay and nothing like it is to be found in the Garvellachs. Watson suggests that the claims of Jura are so strong as to be conclusive. Marsden says "Along the shore of the bag shaped bay on Loch Tarbert are a number of large caves. One of them is known as 'Uaimh mhuinntir Idhe' or 'the cave of the people of Iona,' a name which would confirm it, beyond reasonable doubt as the site of the 'hermitage of Muirbolc-mar.' From the point of that recognition, it would seem that the name Hinba itself points firmly to Jura. Hinba was Adamnan's latin form of the old Irish Inbe, literally 'an incision,' and a term which well describes the great cleft of Loch Tarbert cutting Jura almost in half. To which can be added Professor Watson's discovery of a local tradition calling Jura by the Gaelic name of an t-Eilean Ban 'the Holy Island,' and which can only be interpreted as an allusion to an ancient and especial sanctity."

A further piece of evidence connecting Jura with Columba is that in a graveyard at Tarbert on the eastern coast of that island are the foundations of a long building usually described as a 'Celtic Chapel'. It seems to be an early site and its gaidhlig name is said to be 'Cill Chaluim - chille', meaning Columba's cell or church.

Historians take two widely different views of the appearance of the angel. Finlay argues that Columba did indeed prefer Iogenan and that, as a result of the pressures upon him, he "could have had a vision of this kind which he would certainly have attributed to the guidance of God". Colum Kenny says "Given Aedan's subsequent reputation as a ferocious warrior, sceptics may suggest that the story of the angel was invented to dress up some nastier and more worldly form of compulsion".

Clearly, the decision by Columba was momentous. For a cleric, and especially one who had only been in Scotland for some ten years, to impose his will, by intervention on the ruling families of Dal Riada, makes an enormous statement about his importance among his people. He was about to perform the first consecration of a king in the history of Britain.

Cuimine's account of the words used by Columba leave Aedan and ourselves in no doubt that he is making a portentous political statement. "Make no mistake, Aedan, but believe that, until you commit some act of treachery against me or my successors, none of your enemies will have the power to oppose you. For this reason you must give this warning to your sons, as they must pass it on to their sons and grandsons and descendants so that they may not follow evil counsels and so lose the sceptre of this kingdom from their hands. For whenever it may happen that they do wrong to me or to my kindred in Ireland the scourge that I have suffered for your sake from the angel will be turned by the hand of God to deliver a heavy punishment on them. Men's hearts will be taken from them and their enemies will draw strength mightily against them. He then laid his hand upon his head in blessing and consecrated him". What a statement Columba had made and with the following implications.

First "I have made you king and you are king at my pleasure. If you make a move against me or mine this kingdom will be taken away".

Second "By making you consecrated King of all Dal Riada, I have removed you from the ranks of minor kings or toiseadh. You are now a great king".

The two statements must, in Columba's mind almost have been one. As King of Dal Riada, in Scotland, Aedan had a status at least equal to that of the Irish Dal Riata. Also he was strong enough to move against Columba's own people the Ui Neil and was warned not to do so. In all of this Columba foreshadowed the great Convention of Drum Ceatt in the following year and established his own great political power in both countries.

Drum Ceatt is worth considering in some slight detail as it not only confirmed Columba's political power but also established Aedan in Scotland and defined the extent of the authority of Scottish Dal Riada. Aedan became known as a fierce and successful warrior, but he could not have become so without this tremendous underpinning of his power base.

What was Drum Ceatt? Well, first of all it took place at Drum Ceatt in Ulster near the monastery of Derry, Columba's own foundation. Adamnan refers to it as a 'condictus regum,' a conference of kings. The agenda is recorded in the preface to the Amhra Choluimchille as having three items. The first need not concern us here. Second was the plea for the poets who were under threat of banishment as they were burdensome. Third was the relationship between the Irish and Alban kingdoms of Dalriada, probably strained since Aedan's power had grown. There is a strong case for the third being the only real purpose of the convention.

Columba arrived in company with King Aedan of Alban Dal Riada, and, according to the poet Dallan Forgaill, he had with him a great company.

> Forty priests was their number,
> Twenty bishops, noble, worthy,
> For singing psalms, a practice without blame,
> Fifty deacons, thirty students.

The convention was the arena for a critical confrontation with Aedh, king of the Irish Dal Riata. Columba, a Celtic Prince, was well aware that a meek appearance would count for nothing and that he must present himself with the trappings of regality. Pomp and circumstance would count at such a meeting. He was uniquely placed to provide it with as many recruits as he could use from his own monastery.

We have touched on the proposed banishment of the poets in a previous chapter. Aedh is said to have insisted on their banishment and Columba to have retorted, on behalf of the poets "the praises they will sing for him are enduring for Cormac, grandson of Conn. And the treasures which are given for them were transitory, while the praises live after them" The poets were cheap at the price. Aedh, then relented. Clearly, thus early in the convention, Columba had wrong footed him and so, prepared the ground for the more important debate to come and, according to Bannerman the only reason for which Columba had attended.

The two rulers involved in this "conference of kings", according to Adamnan were Aedh, son of Ainmire, and Aedan, son of Gabran, who attended with Columba. The point at issue was the status of Aedan's new kingdom of Dal Riada in Alba. Until the coming of Columba it had been little more than a province of the Irish Dal Riata, and a shrinking province at that and one under serious threat from the Picts. Columba's positive thinking had transformed that situation. By securing the throne for an able and determined man like Aedan, he had made the province a more effective force than the kingdom from which it sprang. A colony, as Skene emphasised was due to pay a list of tributes as well as to support on the battlefield the superior king.

According to the Amhra Choluimchille, Columba appointed Colman, son of Comgellan, to decide between the claims of the men of Erin and the men of Alba. It is more likely that he in fact appointed Colman to deliver a judgement of Columba's own devising. This was that "Dalriada in Scotland was to be freed from all tribute to the supreme king of Ireland, but that they were to join in expeditions and hostings when called upon with the exception of the sea gatherings and maritime expedition". That meant that Aedan became, virtually, independent of Ireland. Aedan, quite plainly regarded the judgement delivered at Drum Ceatt as a licence not only to consolidate, but to expand his power. The religious and cultural bonds with Ireland were to remain close for centuries and were to determine the ultimate character of Scotland. We can say with certainty that Aedan's military ability together with Columba's political acumen laid a foundation on which the kingdom of Scotland was to be built.

But, it is now in Aedan, grandfather of Molaise, rather than Columba that we are more interested. He was established as a king of mighty consequence whose blood line continues to the present royal family, but also as a great Christian King. This further allows us to assess Molaise's importance both in the Church and personally. We can, now, understand a major reason for his people, the Dal Fiatach asking him to become King. They would be in a position to forge an alliance with the Dal Riada in both Scotland and Ireland and, thus, increase hugely, their own strength and influence. There is no doubt that, added to these political considerations, his reputation as a miracle worker would have made him a man of all qualities and no known weakness. We may conclude that it is a combination of these factors which led to their invitation. After all, how many men have been invited to be king merely on account of their holiness?

Having described the importance of Aedan and Columba in the consideration of the life of Molaise it is worth mentioning that Columba is credited with providing the child with his baptismal name. Columba's own anm-chara, soul friend, had been Lasrein of Innishmurray, a Saint also known as "Molaise" and who was probably involved in Columba's decision to leave Ireland for Iona. Some of our Molaise's time was, as we have seen, spent at his grandfather Aedan's stronghold at Dunadd and with Columba living nearby in Iona, it is quite possible that they met.

We are certain that Molaise met, while a child, with his uncle Blaan (today, Blane) of Bute. Blaan was adopted as patron saint of Dunblane and also has Blanefield and the Blane Valley near Glasgow named after him. The following story of their meeting is told in the Manuscript.

"The revered bishop Blaan, uncle to the child, and hearing of his miracles set out to visit him. While he was being welcomed by the guardians of the child, one of his horses was stolen. On hearing this, Blaan said "He whom we are visiting should either retrieve our horse or provide another". But God heard the word of his servant and made the thief return the horse. Blaan asked him why he had returned the horse and the thief replied "The soldiers of King Cairell are following me so I seek the protection of his son". Blaan gave thanks and returned to Bute. "After this Mathgemm (Gemma) being warned in a vision by an angel took the boy to be educated in his own country by Holy Munnu".

This Munnu is remembered at Kilmun, in the Church of Our Lady and St Mun in Dunoon, the isle of St Munde in Lochleven and at the parish church of St Munn's Glencoe. It was the parish priest of St Munn's, Monsignor Roddie Macdonald, who presented me with a copy of his translation of the Salamanca Manuscript which is mentioned elsewhere in this book. The translation is entitled "ex codice olim Salmanticensi nunc Bruxellensi" indicating that the original which was once in Salamanca is now to be found in Brussels. The frontispiece contains the note "For the use and edification of the pastor of St Munn's parish Glencoe in the Diocese of Argyll and the Isles".

When Molaise had completed his education with Munnu he rejected the approach of his people to make him their king and fled to Arran. There he settled with the intention of, eventually, travelling to Rome to visit the relics of the saints and so we may now consider the life of Molaise in Arran.

His genealogy showing his descent from the ancient kings of Dal Riata is:-

Cairpre Riata then nine generations, then
Fergus Mor mac Erc died 501AD
Domangart died 506AD
Comgall died 540AD
Gabran brother of Comgall died 558AD
Connalgal son of Comgall died 574AD
Aedan mac Gabrain, son of Gabran died 606AD
Gemma daughter of Aedan
Molaise son of Gemma by Cairell King of the Dal Fiatach
and grandson of Aedan mac Gabrain.

CHAPTER 12

molaíse ín arran
ano the holy ísle

Perhaps we should look first at his name. We have noticed that he was called, in Ireland, by their version of his name "Laisren" while, in Scotland, he was Molaise. The derivation of his name is as follows. His baptismal name was "Las" meaning flame or light. The "mo" was used by the Celts as a term of affection and respect and so, added to "Las" meant "My dear Las". We find this form of derivation frequently in Scotland so "Kilmacolm" for example was, originally "Cille mo Colm" meaning "The church of my dear Columba". So we have now identified his name, in Scotland, as "Molas". The "i" came to be added to provide the genitive or owning case so that the Holy Isle was called Eilean Molaise "Isle of Molaise," and the suffix "se" again in Scots gaidhlig, is emphatic; so "me" in English is "mi" but if the speaker wishes to be emphatic and to say "me, not anybody else" he says "mise". Only the "e" was used as the "s" was already there so the whole name became Molaise. The version used in Ireland "Laisren", could just as easily have been used in Scotland as the suffix "en" or "ian" simply means "little".

It is important that his name should not be mispronounced so that we all finish up talking about different people. The pronunciation, phonetically is MO-LASH-EH. The common error of pronouncing it to rhyme with Blaise or laze has caused quite enough confusion as it is!

It is suggested by many historians that he came to the Holy Isle determined to live the life of a hermit or anchorite. If he intended to do this, the evidence suggests that he was, to an extent, unsuccessful. He seems to have been open to visits from the people of the Island at all times and the presence of the "judgement stone" outside his cave suggests that he was accustomed to deciding between causes and dispensing justice for them. In many other respects he truly lived the hermit life - there was, apparently no other person to form a community with him though it is entirely possible that some of the other caves on Holy Isle were also inhabited by hermits. Modern historians take the view that, on deciding to escape from his people and their worldly demands upon him, he elected to become, as Columba before him, one of the "Peregrini", the wanderers who sought "the place of their resurrection". That he did this in a place which was under the control of Dalriadan forces is hardly surprising. We know that he saw Arran as merely a transitional phase in his life.

And now, the fascinating question - "why Arran?". Molaise would certainly have had access to the legends of the old Irish heroes who believed that Arran was the "Land of the blest" and who asserted that it had the best hunting in their world.

The Book of Arran says "Legends of gods and heroes lightly brush its shores. Like some other western isles it figures as the residence of Mannanan mac Lir son of Ler old god of the sea. Mannanan makes his home in Emhain Abhlach - 'Emhain of the apples' where the apples are no passing fruit of an earthly tree but the honey tasted apples of the land of perpetual youth." One identification of this insular paradise fixes it on Arran and the anonymous poet who works the tale into his verses of the eleventh century makes a significant reference:

We will ask a harbour behind Arran,
whilst seeking the cold strands of Erin.

Iarrfam cuan ar cul Arann,
Ag sur traghann nfhuar n' eirionn.

Emhain Abhlach is frequently related by historians to the Arthurian Avalon and the Book of Arran makes the connection with the tale of Arthur's restless eldest brother sweeping down from Scotland to plunder his territories.

A famous legend is that when the old sea god Ler lost his wife, the king of the divine tribe of Danu, the Tuatha de Dannan, gave him choice of his three foster daughters whose mother was Ailoll of Arran.

Molaise may have known the great Celtic myths of Finn or Fingal remembered in Arran by Dun Fionn, and of Ossian whose grave is on Arran and whose Daughter/wife/mistress Malvina is buried on Machrie Moor, the scene of her favourite hunting ground.

He would certainly have been aware that, in one of the great blendings of mythical and real characters, Caeilte, after the battle of Gabhra, is brought to meet St Patrick and his monks who marvel at the sight of the big men and their huge wolf dogs. These men are so tall that when they sit down, the mere mortals reach only to their waist or their shoulder. Patrick asks Caeilte "What was the best hunting that the Fianna ever had either in Ireland or Scotland?" The answer came prompt and short, "The hunting of Arran", "Where is that land" asked Patrick. "Betwixt Scotland and Pictland" Caeilte replied. He then burst forth into a lyric of glorious praise." Arran of the many stags - the sea impinges on her very shoulders! an island in which whole companies were fed - and with ridges among which blue spears are reddened! Skittish deer are on her pinnacles, soft blackberries on her waving heather; cool water there is in her rivers, and mast upon her russet oaks! Greyhounds there were in her and beagles; Blaeberries and sloes of the dark blackthorn; dwellings with their backs set close against her woods, and the deer fed scattered by her oaken thickets! A crimson crop grew on her rocks, in all her glades a faultless grass; over her crags affording friendly refuge leaping went on and fawns were skipping! Smooth were her level spots - her wild swine, they were fat; cheerful her fields (this is a tale that may be credited), her nuts hung on her forest hazels' boughs, and there was sailing of long galleys past her! Right pleasant their condition all when the fair weather sets in: under her rivers' brinks trouts lie; the sea gulls wheeling round her grand cliff answer one the other - at every fitting time delectable is Arran".

What a description! Although there exist many more prosaic reasons for his selecting Arran- the protection of his grandfather's army, the ease of getting to and from Ireland and Dunadd, the fact that, as far as we know, no one else had previously selected the Island as their place of redemption - it is reasonable to believe that his knowledge of these legends had, at least, an influence in his decision.

The Holy Isle fills the entrance to Lamlash Bay so that, from the mainland, it appears as an integral part of Arran with Mullach Mor, its highest point at 1030 feet being just one more peak amongst the many. It has a beauty about it which varies from the stark to the gentle depending on the point of view, the time of day and the weather. To those who live on Arran it is the most often depicted of the scenes which attract the interest of the Island's many artists. Although it is only two miles long, so difficult is the terrain that it can take four hours to walk round it. Its protection has helped turn Lamlash Bay into a safe deep water harbour which has sheltered the battle fleets of the Norsemen and Great Britain. Many picture postcards still exist on Arran which show the Grand Fleet anchored there during the first world war and it was there that the tatters of Haakon's Fleet took refuge after the disasterous battle of Largs in 1263AD. While there, Vigleikr, the King's Marshall, cut his name into the roof of

Runic inscriptions in Molaise's Cave

The cross of unusual design carved
above the cave

Molaise's cave and there are other Runic inscriptions there believed to date
from the eleventh century.

It was in 1908 that J.A.Balfour conducted his survey of the Holy Isle. He
commenced with an attempted excavation of the fortress built by Somerled in
the twelfth century and the monastery built by Reginald MacSomerled, Rex
Insularum in the thirteenth. He says that Molaise's cave was about one mile
from these erections and at the extreme southern tip of the Holy Isle, simply a
long slit in the rock when viewed from the King's Cross shore. Balfour gave the
measurements of the cave as 38 and a half feet long and 13 feet broad at its
widest point. Modern measurement shows him to have been precise. He gave
this description "The cell is paved from the middle to the northeast corner or for
about 26 feet. In this paving is set a large stone raised but little above the paving;
it measures 5 feet 11 inches in length by 1 foot 8 inches in depth; the ends lie

almost north and south. Some of the paving having got shifted an examination was made of the rock below, and a drain was found cut out of the solid rock, it passes out under the flags at the foot of the stair. When about three feet of soil and loose stones had been removed, a deposit of black matter was reached, in which were considerable deposits of shells mostly limpet and oyster. The full significance became obvious when a number of bones were found that had been split to extract the marrow; the mass was simply kitchen refuse. Most of the bones were those belonging to domesticated animals. When the rubbish had been removed a fireplace was brought to view whose vent is made between the courses of stones forming the wall".

The stone which measured 5 feet 11 inches by 1 foot 8 inches is believed by some historians to have been an altar stone but this is unlikely as Molaise was

Molaise's Cave

not ordained priest until he had left Arran and, consequently, would have had no use for an altar. The drain beneath the stone confirms our view that it was a kitchen table as a drain would not have been necessary under an altar. In addition to the shells of limpets and clams there were bones of pigs, young ox, sheep and deer. Balfour also notes the crosses "made by pilgrims and runic inscriptions". Kennedy Cameron says "From Runic inscriptions on the wall of his cell on the Holy Isle it would appear that the place, about the year 1100AD became the abode of a Norwegian hermit. On the shore below the cave is a boulder or stone with a flat top known as the Saint's chair. A holy well is also nearby, celebrated for its healing virtues which are alleged to have been communicated to it by the prayers and blessings of the Saint". This boulder, also known as 'The Judgement Stone' appears to have seats hewn out of its four corners which may be seen easily today. Other names for this stone are the Saint's Table and Pulpit Rock.

Near the cave is, as Kennedy Cameron says, Molaise's well, a clear spring which bubbles out of the hillside. This was thought to bring a blessing to all who drank from it and to cure their ills. It would certainly have been instrumental in determining the Saint's dwelling place. A clear spring in front of

Molaise's Spring or Well

your house would be desirable even today. In front of the Judgement stone is a stone with a circular depression hollowed out of it. Kenny suggests that this may have been the receptacle for "that specially rounded and portable stone which was, traditionally connected with the Saint".

This was described by Martin as follows. "I had like to have forgot a valuable curiosity on this isle which they call Baul Muluy i.e. Molingus, his stone globe, so much esteemed by the inhabitants. This stone for its intrinsic value has been carefully transmitted to Posterity for several Ages. It is a green Stone much like a globe in figure and about the bigness of a Goose Egg. The vertues of it is to remove Stitches from the sides of Sick Persons, by laying it close to the place affected, and if the patient does not outlive the Distemper they say the Stone removes out of the bed of its own accord and, e contra. The natives use this stone for swearing decisive oaths upon it. They ascribe another extraordinary Vertue to it. and 'tis this - the credulous Vulgar firmly believe that

Rock variously know as "Pulpit Rock", "Judgement Stone"
and "Saints Chair" or "Table"

if this stone is cast among the Front of an Enemy, they will all run away, that as often as the enemy rallies, if this stone is cast among them, they will lose courage and retire. They say that Mackdonald of the Isles carried this Stone about with him, and that Victory was always on his side when he threw it among the enemy. The Custody of this Globe is the peculiar privilege of a little family called Clan-Chattons alias Mack Intosh, they were ancient followers of Mack Donald of the Isles. This Stone is now in the custody of Margaret Millar alias Mack Intosh, she lives in Baellmianich, and preserves the globe with abundance of care; it is wrapped up in fair Linen Cloath, and about that is a piece of Woolen Cloath and she keeps it still lock'd up in her chest when it is not given out to exert its qualities.

A further legend concerning the 'healing stone' of St Molaise is still told on the Island. It was the practice of the Saint to take the stone with him when he went to visit the sick. When he entered the room where the afflicted person lay, he laid the stone upon the floor. From its action was indicated what should happen. If it remained stationery the sick person recovered, if it rolled out of the door their death was certain."

Writers on Molaise are agreed that he was of exemplary bearing and showed all the spirituality of the Celtic Church with the single exception of Thomas Headrick who wrote his book "A View of the Island of Arran" in 1807AD. He says of Molaise "I could not help remarking that this Saint, along with many others whom I may have occasion to specify, acquired his celebrity when dirt, nastiness, and absurdity formed the most prominent features of sanctity. Had he chosen a similar cave on the opposite side of this island, where no boat could approach him, and where people from Arran could not get to him without danger of breaking their bones among the loose fragments of rock, with which the beach is encumbered, we might believe him to have retired from the haunts of men in downright earnest. But he chose a residence where the channel is narrowest, and most easily accessible from Arran, and within the bay, where vessels from all quarters would find safety. Hence his object must have been, not to retire from the world but to draw the world after him; and I doubt not but in this cave he displayed more pride, vanity, and pomposity, than Diogenes in his tub, or Bonaparte while seating himself upon a throne".

Headrick is the only writer to portray this point of view. It is, of course, entirely subjective and is emotional at a religious level and, in its concluding sentence displays only religious prejudice, but it raises a valid point. Why did Molaise choose that cave in particular? Well, we note that it had a spring

The Hollow Stone at the foot of the Judgement Stone
which may have contained the Baul Mulay

51

immediately outside. Also we know that ease of access and egress were important to him. In spite of Headrick's odd view that he intended to be the complete anchorite and then chastising him because he didn't measure up to this entirely arbitrary and Headrick imposed condition, we know that he did wish to look after the interests of his people and that, in order to do this they required access to him and he to them.

To put this view of Molaise in context, it is helpful to consider Headrick's view of Columba and his comparison of Molaise and Columba as follows. "The Christian faith appears to have been planted in this island by St Molios, who was a disciple of the celebrated St Colm, or Columba, the apostle of the Highlands and Isles. One cannot read the history of this Saint, as edited by Mr Pinkerton, and more fully illustrated by Dr Smith of Campbelton, without being impressed with a belief that his conduct was not altogether suitable to his profession, or to the transcendent talents with which he was endowed. Though we have only the testimony of an admiring disciple, who would naturally endeavour to keep out of view everything unfavourable to his character, yet even his narrative excites a suspicion that he murdered Oran, on account of some unhappy difference in religious opinion. His zeal against women, whom he would not allow to enter his sacred island, is also liable to suspicion; when it is certain that, in his days, marriage was not considered inconsistent with the character of a clergyman. Though he banished women from his sacred island, he seems to have kept a seraglio of them on a small island adjacent, under the designation of a Nunnery.

After he became old he allowed his women to come to him, in his famous island, to save himself the trouble of going to them. The traditions in Arran state, that Molios, disgusted with the irregularities of his master, withdrew himself from his society and, wishing to support that austerity of manners, which, though not absolutely required in every professor of Christianity, he deemed indispensibly necessary in one who undertook the office of a missionary to convert the heathen, took up his residence in a cave in the island of Lamlash, from him called Holy Island. It appears that, after he had made many converts in Arran, he removed to the district of Shiskin, where he died at the advanced age of 120 years. So Molaise, who in the first excerpt is derided, is held up as a paragon of virtue compared to Columba. Incidentally, for those unfamiliar with the name 'Oran' whom Headrick gratuitously accuses Columba of murdering, there was such a saint whose life is remembered in Saint Oran's chapel on Iona. It was built about the twelfth century and has been much restored since then. His proper name was Odhran and his feast is commemorated on October the 27th. His obituary is entered in the Annals of the Four Masters as 548AD - a full fifteen years before Columba left Ireland. De mortuis nil nisi bonum is not a philosophy which recommends itself to Headrick.

It is difficult to take seriously almost anything that Headrick says, so error strewn is his writing, and a great pity that we cannot as he provides historical detail, unknown to other writers, which would be enormously helpful if it were true. The assertion that Molaise was a disciple of Columba would, in itself, be a gem. He has copied this from Pennant as he does with the Saint's visits to and death in Shiskine and quotes him frequently throughout his book and, therein lies the root of his problem. The confusion betwen Molaise and Molios which Headrick makes was begun by Pennant in his 'Tour to the Hebrides', written in 1774 (Headrick's book was published in 1807) of which, more anon.

The Holy Isle was known, in Molaise's day as Eilean Molaise and this name became, by corruption, the name of the village on the shore - Lamlash. The island was, again according to Kennedy Cameron, "known to the Norsemen as Malassey. The term was, no doubt, at first applicable to the Island only. It was Eilean Molaisi. The bay and district were spoken of in gaidhlig as Loch-an-Eilean or Loch of the Island". Boyd Scott in his book "The East of Arran" published in 1919 is able to speak in the present tense and say "People hereabouts who speak gaelic still refer to the Holy Isle as Eilean Molaise; and when they speak of going to Lamlash they say they go to Loch-an Eilean, which means Loch of the Island". Fordun, writing in the fourteenth century, gives the name as Almeslache which, as Professor McKinnon points out suggests the steps by which the change has taken place in the name. Eilean Molaisi became Elmolaisi, then Lamolash, now Lamlash. Boyd Scott prefers Eilean Molaise, 'Lan Molaise then Lanmolash, and then Lamlash.'.

Donald Munro, Dean of the Isles, in "A description of the western Isles of Scotland called Hybrides" in 1549 says "with ane ither litle ile callit the yle of Molass quherin ther was foundit by John, Lord of the isles ane monastery of friars which is decayit".

The Holy Isle was, as we know, used up until the end of the 18th century as a burial ground but, at that time, a boat carrying a party of mourners went down in a great storm and many were drowned. It was this use that Mr and Mrs Morris were attempting to revive in the 1980's. One of the delightful legends of Arran runs that, when the people were attempting to find a successor burial ground they followed a mysterious light which led them to some land round the Church of Kilbride.

There seems to have been quite a habit, in Arran, of continuing to use the old graveyards even when the building associated with them had gone and certainly when the church might have been expected to disapprove. On the far side of the Island, at Sliddery, St Mary's Churchyard was used for burials by local people long after the church itself had been relocated.

In 1860, the stone cross, known as Brigid's Cross was removed from the cemetery on the Holy Isle and buried in the grounds of the Old Kilbride Parish Church in Lamlash and it is easy to visualise the folk of the Island making the connection that if they had had to move the burial ground then they should bring the Cross to the new one. In 1892 it was disinterred and erected in front of the present parish church of Kilbride. It has been pointed out that this is almost certainly the same cross that had stood, originally, at Cnoc na Croise and had given that place its name. There are many questions about its probable age. It is not a Celtic Cross and the carving of Christ's body disappearing into a chalice and the blood flowing from the chalice to a supplicant below seems to make it mediaeval and not a little barbaric. None of this makes it unauthentic. Many aspects of the Church in Arran including the formation of the parishes of Kilbride and Kilmory came into being in the 13th and 14th centuries. The carving of St Molios at Shiskine is also from this time when great reverence was shown to the Celtic Saints. It was probably erected centuries after Molaise when Cnoc na Croise was an important part of the Pilgrim's Way and would have marked the point at which pilgrims travelling from the west of the Island would have caught their first glimpse of the Holy Isle.

St. Brigid's Cross in the grounds of
Lamlash Parish Church

CHAPTER 13

molaise and molios

Having mentioned the name of Molios of Shiskine, it is appropriate to consider the great debate as to whether they were one and the same person or two completely different people. We have noted that one of the first writers to comment was Thomas Pennant in 1774. Pennant was unusual in that he made a point of travelling to any location which interested him and taking views from the people first hand and recording their oral traditions. For this, he must be greatly honoured and his work valued. As a result of his methodology, his work is mainly anecdotal and his book is entitled "A tour to the Hebrides". He does not pretend to be a historian, but he has the virtue that it is anecdotal at first hand and, accordingly was able to expand the view of subsequent writers. Unfortunately, few of them could test his writing with the sort of facilities which are available today and in some cases like Headrick, swallowed him whole. On the subject of Molios Pennant says "In Shiskin or Seasgain churchyard is a tomb called that of Maol-Jos, that is 'The servant of Jesus'. The Saint is represented in the habit of a priest with a chalice in his hands and a crozier by him. The stone was broken about half a year ago by some sacriligious fellow in search of treasure. An islander who stood by me assured me that the attempt did not go unpunished as soon afterwards, the audacious wretch was visited with a broken leg. Saint Maol-Jos was a companion of Saint Columba who chose Iona as the place of his residence. Maol-Jos fixed on the little island of Lamlash and officiated by turns at Shiskin where he died at the age of a hundred and was there interred".

We find four points of difficulty with Pennant's account.

Firstly "and officiated by turns at Shiskin". This could not refer to Molaise who was not ordained while in Arran and so could not have "officiated" anywhere.

Second, having correctly identified the Saint of Shiskine as Molios meaning "servant of God", he is not aware that the Saint of Holy Isle has an entirely different name whose derivation we know.

Third, Molaise died at Leighlin, in Ireland on the 18th of April 639 or 640 AD and was no older than 74 and may have been as young as 67. His death and funeral are well documented. This, however was information to which Pennant had no access any more than did the folk of Shiskine and so the error was proliferated. It is right to mention, here, the accounts of his death and funeral. In the martyrology of Oengus dating from the 10th century, his death is entered as 18th April which is kept as his feast day in both Scotland and Ireland. This coincides with the Martyrology of Donegal which gives precisely the same information but adds "Molaise was of the race of Fiatach Finn, King of the Erin, of the seed of Heremon"

Fourth, "was a companion of Saint Columba". Molios was certainly not "a companion of Saint Columba" who had died in 597AD and Molios lived in the 13th century. It is also extremely unlikely that Molaise was "a companion of Saint Columba" although there is no doubt that he knew him as has been mentioned elsewhere in this book.

On the feast day of Septimus,
A noble deacon,
Laisren victorious flame,
gentle abbot of Lethglenn,
died and gone to heaven.

During his lifetime, he had asked Saint Maignen to oversee his funeral. This was a remarkable and important event. A life of Maignen recorded in the British Library MS says "Accordingly, Maignen carried out the order of these obsequies which made the third most exalted funeral in Ireland: Patrick at Dun da leth nglas (Downpatrick), Mochuda in Rath of O suanaig and Molasius that by Holy Maignen was buried".

No-one disagrees that Molaise was indeed Abbot of Leighlin and died there, nor does anyone quote any account of his body or any part of it being removed, after his death, to Shiskine. There can be no doubt that the Saint buried in Clauchan Glen was indeed Molios and of a much later date than Molaise. There was a holy well, near both Clauchan and Shiskine named after him. There seems little doubt that the confusion, in the Arran folk memory arises first from the similarity of the two names and it must be remembered that this occurred at a time when spelling was, in any event, unreliable and, second, from the existence of the Pilgrim's way which we will examine later.

Our fourth observation on Pennant's account must be on the statement that he was "a companion of Columba". It is, as we note elsewhere, entirely probable that he knew Columba but to state with any accuracy that he was a companion of the great Saint we would require evidence of a length of relationship that so far has not been produced. Again Pennant is listening to local lore.

Naturally, the old historians of Arran come down on one side or the other. McArthur noted in 1873; "The old churchyard (at Clauchan) still remains with its primitive tombstones. Near its centre is the tomb of St Molios whose tombstone is said to have been brought from Iona, sculptured with the figure of the Saint arrayed in the robes of a mitred abbot with pastoral staff by his side and chalice in his hands. There is nothing improbable in the suggestion that the body of Saint Molios may have been brought from Ireland to the island where

The Gravestone of Molios at Clauchan shown in situ

he is said to have passed the early years of his manhood and been buried there in the little secluded cemetery of the Clauchan. The Arran people fondly cling to the time honoured traditions of their patron saint and we would not rudely strip from the old burial place the sacred association which has consecrated the dust of so many generations". The last sentence indicates a certain cynicism on McArthur's part about the story he is relating. "We would not rudely strip" although, perhaps in the interests of accuracy we ought to. The stone may indeed have come from Iona but we know that it was carved in the style of a 12th - 13th century bishop and is unrelated to the Celtic carvings of the 6th and 7th centuries. Significantly, McArthur produces no evidence on these points but remarks "There is nothing improbable in the suggestion." No indeed. There is simply no evidence to suggest that it actually happened!

On the other side of the argument is Kennedy Cameron in 'The Church in Arran'. "This early Christianity is closely associated with the Holy Isle which guards the entrance to Lamlash Bay and with the Saint Molash. Molash was born in Ireland in 566AD. He was educated in Bute. At the age of 20 he retired to the Holy Isle where the cell in which he lived is still to be seen......he afterwards returned to Ireland where, in 614AD he was elected abbot of Leighlin. He died in 640AD."

Apart from the statement "He was educated in Bute", this is the orthodox story of Molaise. Did his uncle Blaan have a hand in his education? We know that he visited Molaise but the impression given by the Salamanca Manuscript is that it was a visit of short duration. However, having visited him once it is possible that Blaan renewed the acquaintanceship on other occasions and that, on at least some of these he took a hand in his nephew's education. There is, however apart from Kennedy Cameron, no other mention of Molaise visiting Bute.

Another learned commentator on this question, and one who sees both sides of it is Dr Alexander Cameron of Kilbride. He maintains that "It is not correct to claim, as is done in the Originales Parochiales that the Saint's name is the same as Maeljos or Molios, the name of the reputed Saint of Shisken. Maeljos or Maelisi means an attendant or servant of Jesus; whereas Molash or Molaisi means "my flame". The possessive pronoun "mo" is often used in gaelic with the names of saints as an endearment. The traditional belief is that the names of Molash or Molaisi are names of one and the same person, that he carried out evangelising work both at Lamlash and at Shisken and that he was buried at Clachan. It is possible that this tradition may be true for Molash, a term of endearment, may be the proper name of the Saint and Molios his ecclesiastical name. There are various examples in gaelic literature of a similar application of terms to popular preachers such as Mo Gradh, Mo Laogh etc. A somewhat analagous case is that of Maolrubha who was also known as the Sagart Ruadh. The death and burial of Molios or Molash having taken place at Shisken would seem to militate against him being the same person as Molash who was abbot of Leighlin and afterwards became a bishop. It would rather appear to indicate that he was a different person whose labours were confined to Arran and who died there as tradition alleges. A monumental effigy which was found in the Clachan burying ground and which has been built into the front wall of the present mission church at Shisken is said to be a statue of St Molios. The vestments, however, show that the ecclesiastical is not of the Celtic Church but of mediaeval times. It is, therefore, not that of the Saint in question, or, if it is, it was carved at a later time when mediaevalism had laid hold of the Island".

Dr Alexander Cameron seems with his statement to have summed up the case with great clarity. Two points emerge from his summary. It is possible, as he speculates, that one holy man could have had both a personal and an ecclesiastical name. Some gaidhlig scholars suggest that any monk might have been referred to as Maol Iosa or Molios - the tonsured one of Jesus. This is true and, in addition we know of the habit of giving spiritual people a baptismal and also a clerical name. Columba for example was christened with one name, probably Criomhthann and was only later entitled Columcille or Dove of the Church. Unfortunately there is not one reference in any document to Molaise by any name other than Molaise or Laisren. These are the only names by which he was known either in his own day or later.

Balfour in 'The Book of Arran' is decisive. Referring to the effigy of Molios on the Stone in Shiskine Churchyard he says "That this effigy has no connection with Molaise the hermit saint of the Holy Isle there can hardly be any doubt. St Molaise became abbot of Leighlin in Ireland, and there he died (see Acta Sanctorum). Local tradition has it that the effigy represents the saint and it is perhaps not difficult to see how the popular idea has arisen. The confusion is between the names Maol-Iosa (contracted form Molios), 'The tonsured for Jesus' and Molaise, Mo (a suffix of endearment) Las or Laise, flame or brightness, a poetical phrase indicating 'my dear one' or 'my bright joy'. The term Maol-Iosa was very fitting for the effigy in question, when the name of the eccliastic represented had been forgotten. The sound of the names in speech is not so widely different as to prevent misunderstanding. Briefly, then, the stone that was with haste lifted from Clauchan Churchyard and set in cement in the wall of the chapel is but the monumental effigy of an unknown saint or sinner." This observation by Balfour reflects the point made above that any monk could have been referred to as Maol-Iosa especially if his proper name was no longer remembered. Certainly, the more evidence that is gathered on this Maol-Iosa, the more it appears likely that this was just a generic name.

Our problems with the theory that Molaise and Molios are the same person are many. It rests, as we have noted on too much conjecture and too little examination of the evidence. The 18th and 19th century commentators fall into two classifications; those who believe that they are two different people and those who are unaware that any question exists. The difficulty experienced by some, more recent commentators who go for the 'one and the same' theory is that they seem to believe that the early 'don't knows' support the 'same person' school of thought whereas they are simply unaware that the question exists and, like McArthur, invent ingenious explanations for the paradoxes involved in the Saint's apparent ability to be in two places at once and to die in two different places and at two different ages.

We are plagued by the 'ifs'. 'If' the monks of Leighlin were willing to give up the body of their beloved founder and abbot, which is so unlikely that, had it occurred, it must have been the subject of some comment. Why is there none? In an otherwise well documented life, death and burial, there is simply no mention of it. 'If' his body was translated from Leighlin to Shiskine, why is there no record of its happening and why is there no mention of it in the folk history of Shiskine gleaned by Pennant? It was, after all, a hugely significant event had it occurred and could not fail to have been mentioned in either the written or the oral tradition or both. 'If' we accept that a mediaeval stone was meant to depict a monk of the Celtic Church then we have to remember that, even if it was carved in mediaeval times, they were aware what a Celtic monk had looked like and, had they intended to depict one, they were well able to do so. The reason is that the folk of Arran were simply unaware of the dichotomy and, therefore, found no necessity to invent an explanation.

Undoubtedly, there existed at Shiskine in mediaeval times a monk known as Molios who must have been an abbot or bishop, or for that matter, as indicated by the mitre and crozier on the gravestone, both. Importantly, Molaise, while on Arran, was neither. Molios was a man of great holiness and piety and much loved by the community. Such was their love for him and their memory of that love that their successors in the 19th century went to very great lengths to preserve his image and this, at a time when saints and their images

St Molios Church as Clauchan with its pyramydic roof C 1900

Clauchan Church as it is today

were hardly the most welcome of concepts within the Presbyterian Church. The existence of this love and the coincidence of the names has caused a great muddying of the waters over the years. Many historians believe him to have been a monk from Saddell in Argyll which was a Cistercian Abbey which had been granted "the lands of Shisken" in the 13th century which adds much weight to this belief. The chapel which still exists, though in a ruined state, within the Clauchan Cemetery was almost certainly the place where Molios celebrated his services. It appears on both Bleau's and Pont's maps which means that it existed before 1650. This being so, it is likely that it is pre-reformation as new churches were almost unheard of between the mid 16th and the mid 17th centuries. A photograph of that Church taken in the present day is included together with an older version taken when it still possessed its roof. An additional photograph shows the "Lepers Hole" in the wall of the Church and Arran tradition has it that Lepers or other diseased people had to obtain the Sacrament by thrusting their arms through this hole so that they would not contaminate the congregation.

Lepers' Hole through which diseased people thrust their arms to receive the sacrament so that they would not contaminate the congregation

the pilgrim's way

An important factor in confusing Molios with Molaise was the tradition of the existence of a 'Pilgrim's Way' between Shiskine and Lamlash. This was said to be the route followed by Molaise in going from Holy Isle to his 'chapel' in Clauchan. This route and its attribution to Molaise journeying to this 'chapel' presupposes that he ever made the journey or, indeed that he had a chapel in Clauchan. As has been noted earlier, he was not ordained while on Arran and, accordingly could not officiate at any chapel. He was attempting to live the life of a hermit on Holy Isle and is unlikely to have wandered the Island in this way but there is good reason to believe that a 'Pilgrim's Way' or something very like it once existed. Most probably the route was from West to East rather than vice versa. It may have begun at Shiskine, followed the Clauchan Water up the glen and continued to Cnoc na Croise, Lag na Croise and down the Benlister burn to Lamlash. The existence of Cnoc na Croise and Lag na Croise would, otherwise, have to be explained. They would not have been so named without good reason. There still exists in the West of Arran a folk memory of something like a Pilgrim's Way. It is possible that it came into being while the Saint was living in Arran. Equally, it may not have been until mediaeval times and the confusion with Molios may be seen to support this, later, dating.

There is. however, another possibility as to the routing of a Pilgrim's Way. This derives from a well established route in the 19th century of men from Ireland making their way to Glasgow to find work. They landed at Sliddery in the south west of the Island and journeyed to Lamlash which was then the main Island port to take ship for the city. The name 'Sliddery' gives us some help, its derivation is, in gaidhlig, Slidhe an Righ or Slidhe na Righ, meaning "the Lord's or King's Road" which carries you on to Gleann Righ "the Lord's or King's Glen" and so onto the Pilgrim's Way and by following the Burican water across to Cnoc na Dail, Cnoc na Croise, Lag na Croise and so down the Benlister Burn to Lamlash. In those days there was of course no Ross or String Road across the Island and these ancient routes must be seen in that context. There is the possibility that, this latter, was the more commonly used Pilgrim's Way and, certainly, the place names along the way are persuasive, the Hill of the Meeting, the Hill of the Cross, the Hollow of the Cross are all easily associated with pilgrims. Of course, it may be that it was one Pilgrim's Way but with two entrances from the west coast, one at Sliddery and one at Shiskine.

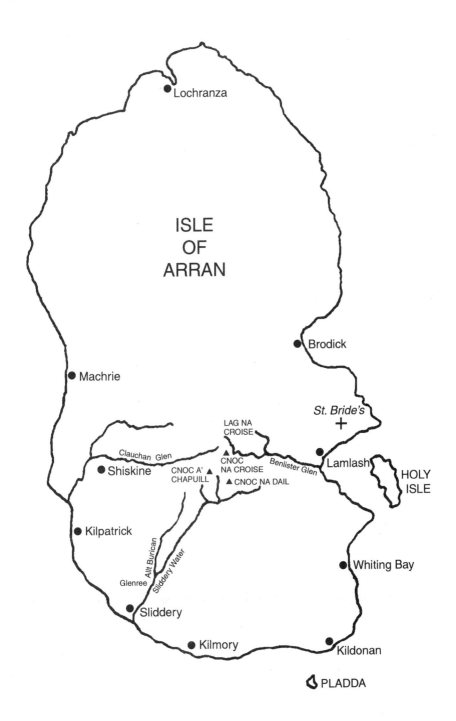

ISLE
OF
ARRAN

Lochranza

Brodick

Machrie

St. Bride's

LAG NA
CROISE

Clauchan Glen

CNOC
NA CROISE

Benlister Glen

Lamlash

Shiskine

CNOC A'
CHAPUILL

CNOC NA DAIL

HOLY
ISLE

Kilpatrick

Allt Burican

Sliddery Water

Glenree

Whiting Bay

Sliddery

Kilmory

Kildonan

PLADDA

CHAPTER 15

molaíse anò
some celtíc saínts

One of the most fascinating questions which the story of Molaise raises is - did he ever meet Columba? One can only state the possibilities created by the circumstancial evidence.

Firstly, we know that their lives overlapped, Columba 521 to 597AD and Molaise, at the narrowest calculation, 573 to 639AD. So the overlap was for a minimum of twenty four years. Secondly, Iona and Arran were sufficiently close geographically for journeys between the two islands to have been made with comparative ease. Thirdly, we know that Blaan, Molaise's uncle, visited Molaise and also met Columba. Fourthly, it is probable that Columba was responsible for naming Molaise after his own anm chara Laisren of Innishmurray. Fifthly, the relationship between Columba and Molaise's grandfather Aedan whom he had consecrated King was a strong and, latterly, very cordial one and became even stronger after the convention of Drum Ceatt. It seems unlikely that Columba would not have met the grandson of his friend and ally who lived so close to him. Sixthly, the Salamanca Manuscript tells us that Columba and other holy men asked Molaise to go to Rome so they were in touch with each other. Seventh and most enticing is the possibility that Columba visited Arran. There are two places on the Island named after him. One is Saint Columba's well at Thunderguy - Tobar Challuim Chille and the other is Suidhe Challuim Chille - Saint Columba's Seat. Significantly this, latter, exists in Gleann an t-Suidhe - Glen of the Seat. This means that, at least at the time that it was named, the local people felt that Saint Columba's Seat was of sufficient consequence to entitle the whole glen after it. It indicates a very powerful attachment to the belief that Columba had rested there while in Arran. There is, however, no documentary evidence that Columba ever made such a visit.

Finally, Molaise's tutor was Fintan Munnu who, in turn, was educated by Columba. The Manuscript tells us "After this Munnu came to the school of Columcille which was in Cille mor Dithrib - in County Roscommon in Ireland - and studied scripture there with Columcille. One day, Columcille sang and when he was finished said 'Who was sitting next to me when I was singing the words of the Holy Script?' And Bithin answered him 'That boy, the son of Tulchan was next to you at your right hand side.' Then Columcille said 'He will be a master of the spiritual life and the most learned by far of this school.'

This relationship with Columba is important because it allows us to position Molaise in regard to other Celtic Saints of his time. The relationships with Munnu and Blaan have been discussed and were common to Molaise and Columba, but Columba had met Saint Mungo about the year 600AD when Molaise according to the dating described above would be about twenty three and living on the Holy Isle. Mungo was, perhaps, after Columba, the most important Celtic saint of his time and in his lasting effect on Scotland. Alexander Gits writing in his 'Life of St Mungo or Kentigern' written in 1967 says "Towards the end of Kentigern's life there took place the memorable meeting with his fellow apostle, the abbot Columba. The two great leaders had apparently, never met before. The abbot of Iona on one of his many expeditions among the Picts, probably in the Kingdom of Fife, had met a party of monks from Glasgow. As a result of this meeting, Columba resolved to pay a visit to the venerable bishop. He and his followers, therefore, crossed the Forth and began their journey southward. Kentigern, hearing of his approach, was filled with joy and prepared to give a great welcome to his brethern from the north. The Gaelic speaking visitors at length came down the hill on the west bank of the Molendinar chanting their latin hymns and the Welsh speaking monks of Glasgow sang their responses in the same common language. The two champions of the Lord, Kentigern and Columba, embraced one another with tears of joy and exchanged croziers in token of fraternal union. The meeting place of the two Saints is marked by St Mungo's well, which may still be seen in a vennel between the new Saracen's Head Inn and the original Inn, now a tenement in Gallowgate."

Jocelyn's earlier account gives the place of the meeting as Mellindonor and comments that "after a spiritual banquet of divine words they refreshed themselves with bodily food then, saying farewell with mutual love they returned to their homes never to meet again." Jocelyn also mentions that Columba's crozier was preserved afterwards in the church of St Wilfrid at Ripon. Given the part that Wilfrid was to play at the Synod of Whitby this was a fine example of the cynicism of fate. Adamnan tells us of the friendship between Columba and Rydderch Hael, King of Strathclyde who was Kentigern's patron and that monks came from Iona to Rydderch's capital at Dumbarton so that the probability of this meeting between the two great Celtic Saints is further substantiated.

A contemporary of Molaise was Donan or Donnan, remembered in Arran at Kildonan where he may have lived at one time. Donan was well known in northern and western parts of Scotland but was specially identified with the Island of Eigg. He was abbot of the monastery there. Kennedy Cameron says that he was slain there about the year 616AD. Lacey says "In 617 during Virgno's period in office (as abbot of Iona), the annals describe the 'burning of Donnan of Eigg on the fifteenth of the Kalends of May (17th April) with one hundred and fifty martyrs'. Eigg is a small island away to the north of Iona and the Ardnamurchan Peninsula. We are unsure about the connections between the church on Eigg and the monastery on Iona. Adamnan, in his description of the three days and nights during which Columba received his vision on Hinba, mentions that, on at least one occasion before 597AD 'Baithin was detained on Eigg by contrary winds' We do not know if he was carrying out some sort of business there or simply sheltering from a storm". There is no satisfactory explanation for the martyrdom of Donnan but the story illustrates some of the dangers encountered by the 'pilgrim monks'. Donnan is said to have been Irish and a number of late sources including the Martyrology of Oengus, purport to give an account of his death.

"It was that Donnan who went to Columcille to seek him as a soul friend, But Columcille said to him, 'I will not be a soul friend to a community of red (blood) martyrdom for you will come to red martyrdom and your brethren with you' and so it happened. Donnan then went with his community to the Hebrides, and they set up their settlement there, where the queen of the country had her sheep. The queen was told this. 'Kill them all,' she said. But everyone said this would not be a very good thing to do. However, they came to kill them. At that time, the cleric was at mass. 'Leave us in peace until the mass is finished,' said Donnan. 'Leave them,' (the killers) said. And when the mass was ended every one of them was slain." There is, however, a number of references to clerics on Eigg in the 8th century, implying the continuation of some kind of church presence there.

Did Molaise ever meet Donan? Did Donan ever visit Arran? We cannot answer these questions but it is fair to say that, of the place names in Arran beginning with 'Kil', Patrick was never at Kilpatrick, Mary at Kilmory, Michael at Kilmichael, Brigid at Kilbride and there is no evidence that Donan was ever at Kildonan. The prefix Kil is derived from the gaidhlig Cill and Cille which are, in turn, derived from the latin cella. In many cases, throughout the Celtic countries, the use of this prefix implies that a monk had his cell at that spot, although it had a more general use. Columba's title Coluimchille meant 'dove of the church' meaning the church in general. Later, it came to mean simply that a church was dedicated at that place to that holy person. In speaking of a wider church, the word eaglais from the latin ecclesia (french eglise) was latterly used. Today, in Scots gaidhlig you would be asked "am bi thu a dol dh'an eaglais Di Domhnaich?" meaning "are you going to church on Sunday?" and the word Cill has reverted to a more specific usage.

molaíse anꝺ
the ꝺate of easter

Although Molaise was educated by Fintan Munnu and would, accordingly, have absorbed the great teacher's views on the date of Easter, he also visited Rome twice. Visits to Rome and the coming under pressure to conform and to adopt the Roman position had changed the views of almost all the Celtic Churchmen who had journeyed there and, with this knowledge, we must wonder at Columba's urging him to go. Wilfrid of Ripon who played such a huge part in the Synod of Whitby is a prime example of this 'conversion'. In any event, Molaise visited Rome twice. On the first occasion he was ordained priest by Pope Gregory the Great and, on the second, he was consecrated bishop by Honorius the first. These visits saw him change sides in the great debate. His affiliation to the Roman side saw him participate with his erstwhile teacher in one of the great meetings on the subject. The Manuscript says "One time there was a great meeting of the people of Ireland on the plain of Ailbe and there was much argument for a whole year over the old Easter and the new Easter. For Laserian of Leighlin with all his followers supported the new order whereas the 'seniores' of Ireland were for the old Easter and the old order. St Munnu did not come immediately to this assembly and they were all waiting for him. For he was the principal defender of the old system. Then Suibhue MacDonail, king of Ui Bairrche said 'Why wait such a long time for that leprous cleric? Even if he does come the Easter order of Laserian will prevail till judgement day.' Laserian said to him 'Be quiet because Munnu hears what you are saying wherever he is and you'll get your comeuppance from him' (did he really say that?). That very day, before vespers Munnu came to the meeting and he and Laserian greeted each other. When king Suibhue asked a prayer from Munnu, the Saint replied 'Why do you ask a prayer from a leprous cleric? When you spoke insultingly about me, Christ at the Father's right hand was ashamed for I am a true member of Christ. Therefore, before the end of the harvest, you will die and your brother will kill you and your blood will be mixed with water and your head will be thrown into the River Barrow and will never be found'. And so it happened. For in that very month his nephew killed him beside a small stream called Blathach, and his head, eventually was swept into the river Barrow.

The next day Munnu said to Laserian in the presence of all the people "It is time, now, to bring this meeting to an end and let everybody go back home. And so, to be brief, I say three things to Laserian. Let two of our books be put in the fire, a book of the old order and one of the new, that we may see which one escapes being burnt. Or else let two of our monks be shut up in the same house which will then be set on fire, to see which one will come safe from the fire. Or, let the two of us, myself and Laserian go to the grave of any worthy monk and let us resurrect him that he may tell us which Easter is being celebrated in heaven this year." To which Laserian replied, "I will not compete against this unreasonable man of God, because, on account of the magnitude of your labours, if you were to say that Slieve Mairge and the plain of Ailbe were to change places, God would do that for you." Then Munnu said "Let each one do what he believes and thinks to be right."

It is evident that Molaise had no doubt on the correctness of his position on the date of Easter but, equally, he had no desire to get into a miracle working contest with his old master. Significantly, with the debate involving two Celts, they were prepared, as always, to agree to disagree. The attitude of the Celtic Church, over the years, had been a mystification as to why the matter was so creakingly important to the Romans and an even greater incredulity that it was important to the Roman Church to inflict its views on others, particularly themselves. The date, as Coleman was to say later, at Whitby, had been handed down from John and that, for them, was good enough. One suspects that the actual date became less important to them, eventually, than a desire not to be directed by people whose ultimate authority, vested in the Pope, they did not acknowledge. In the same way, it was to the Roman Church a political question of paramount importance; it could not permit a church so puny to be seen to be able to flout an establishment whose ultimate aim was to become, in religious terms, the universal authority. This is not to say that the Celts thought that they could impose their views on Rome. It simply didn't occur to them as being all that important.

CHAPTER 17

cbaracter of molaíse

Frequently, one is asked about Molaise, "Can you see his face?" to which the answer has to be "No". His personality has to be constructed from his actions and how he related to other people. His early miracles have been described here and some later ones occurring in Ireland, are worth mentioning to round out that aspect of the man. The Manuscript provides the following, 'A certain woman, carrying in her arms the body of her son who had been beheaded by robbers, earnestly entreated Saint Lasrianus to restore him to life. His feelings of pity were stirred by the lamentations of the mother and he turned to his usual help of prayer and, having placed the head beside the body he restored the dead man to life and gave him back safe to his mother.'

When he tried to buy a piece of land suitable for his monastery at Leighlin, the owner's offer was as much land as could be covered by his cloak. 'The Saint placed his cloak on the ground and it spread outwards till it covered the necessary amount of land for a suitable site.'

When he was visited by St Finbar of Cork he was asked for 'some sign as a memento of our pact' Lasrianus replied "Ask and God will grant it to you" Finbar said "You should ask as we have come to you". Saint Lasrianus prayed and, at once, a bush produced nuts in abundance from which the cross placed there is named.

From these tales we observe a sympathetic and kindly man but, in the book of Leinster, we are provided with a different side to his character. I give here an abridged version of a fairly lengthy account. Molaise's sister who was a nun at Leighlin became pregnant by a monk. Molaise was informed and said "May it be a labour of sudden death then." Thereupon 'he takes away heaven and earth from her.' He would not allow her to be buried in the churchyard and so she was buried in the bog. The young monk, who had fled to Armagh learnt of all this and said, every day, seven 'Beati' the three fifties (all one hundred and fifty psalms) and performed one hundred genuflections. He returned to Leighlin and begged Molaise for a small hut where he might beseech God. Eventually, he saw her in a vision and she told him she was almost saved. "What has saved you most?" asked the young cleric. "The Beati", she answered. Eventually, Molaise saw a ministration of angels rising from the grave towards heaven. He then caused the body to be taken from the bog and buried in the graveyard. The account concludes 'Therefore it is that the Beati is better than all prayers.'

As with Columba and Fintan Munnu, the impression we receive is of a man at once empathic and severe and, although referred to posthumously as 'the gentle abbot' this is clearly a hagiographical statement. Gentle and strict by turns may be as close as we can get from the story of his life. Without doubt he was a true Celt. His pervading need to be close to nature, his spring of crystal clear water, his dwelling on the side of a hill, all give us a feel for the inner man. His flight from worldly appointment and his preference for solitude are qualities by which we can immediately assess him. The son of a king and the grandson of another who, like Christ, turned from these earthly values to a much deeper estimation of the value of his life. A chief disputant in the greatest ecclesiastical question of his day who could agree to differ where what counted was that true unity so beloved of the Celtic Church - its judgement being 'if it might rend us apart then leave it be'. Perhaps his greatest quality is that, having inspired the people of Arran and Leinster in the 6th and 7th centuries AD he is today the same inspiration to the contemplative as well as to a wider public.

The day on which the Samye Ling Tibetan Buddhists took possession of the Holy Isle was on his birthday, 18th April 1992 and this was no mere coincidence. The feelings of the community of Samye Ling are very clear and their identification with his spiritual approach run very deep. At an inter faith service on 22nd April Akong Ripoche, abbot of Samye Ling said "You should not worry that Tibetans are going to lock you out of Holy Isle. It was locked until we came". Abbot Donald McGlynn of the Cistercian Abbey of Nunraw spoke of the parallel monastic tradition in Buddhism and Roman Catholicism and said that he was indebted to the monks of Samye Ling for bringing the Holy Isle to new life.

There is no doubting the spiritual and very personal relationship which the Buddhist Community, especially on the Holy Isle, feel for Molaise. In a conversation with Lama Yeshe Losal, he revealed that, just as the name Molaise is, as we have previously noted, derived from the root "Las" meaning "light or flame", so his own name has precisely the same root and exactly the same meaning. Is this a coincidence? To illustrate that the spiritual comprehension and identification with Molaise went much further, he was able to mention that the Buddhists had, recently, made two purchases in Ireland.

The first was of Kilmainham House outside Dublin. Kilmainham is derived from Cille Maignenn, "The church of Maignenn" who was, as we know, the person charged by Molaise with arranging his obsequies. He arranged for Molaise a funeral which was the third biggest held in Ireland up to that point.

The second purchase was at Leighlinn itself, the site of Molaise's Monastery and the scene of his death and burial where a small piece of ground was acquired to maintain the spiritual relationship more closely. This latter, particularly would be very much in keeping with the traditions of the Celtic Church bearing in mind its strong connection with the earth and nature. It was impossible not to feel that this formed a series of coincidences and a spiritual attitude not capable of some trite explanation.

The Abbot of Samye Ling has indicated that those with an interest in Molaise who wish to visit Holy Isle will be welcome to do so by arrangement. The Tibetans have made it clear that the tradition of the Holy Isle as a place of retreat and contemplation set by Molaise at the end of the 6th century and its ancient spiritual role were compelling reasons for their choosing it. It now houses an inter faith centre for peace, reconciliation and retreat. Truly, the spirit of Molaise lives on!

Bibliography

A.Alfoldi	The Conversion of Constantine and Pagan Rome, 1948
Rev. J. Kennedy Cameron	The Church in Arran 1912
David Ewing Duncan	The Calendar, London, 1998
A.A.M.Duncan	The Making of the Kingdom, Edinburgh, 1974
rep. Felinfach	Annals of Tigernach, 1993
Ian Findlay	Columba, London, 1979
Alexander Gits S.J.	Life of St Mungo or Kentigern, 1967
Thomas Headrick	The Island of Arran, Edinburgh, 1807
R.Hutton	The Pagan Religions of the Early British Isles, Oxford, 1991
A.H.M.Jones	Constantine and the conversion of Europe,1948
Colum Kenny	Molaise, Abbot of Leighlin and Hermit of Holy Island, Ireland, 1998
Brian Lacey	Colum Cille and the Columban Tradition, Dublin, 1997
John McArthur	Antiquities of Arran, 1872
McKenzie MacBride	Arran of the Bens, the Glens, & the Brave, Edinburgh 1910
Robert McLellan	The Isle of Arran, Newton Abbot, 1970
R.McMullan	Constantine,1970
Alan Macquarrie and E. Mairi Macarthur	Iona Through the Ages, 1992
Helen McSkimming	Dal Riata, from Erin to Alba, Arran, 1997
John Marsden	Sea Road of the Saints, Edinburgh, 1995
M.A.Martin	Description of the Western Isles of Scotland, Edinburgh, 1981
Donald Monro Dean of the Isles	Description of the Western Isles of Scotland called Hybrides, 1549
D.M.Nicol	The Immortal Emperor, 1992
John Julius Norwich	Byzantium
Thomas Pennant	Scotland, and A tour to the Hebrides, 1874
Boyd Scott	The East of Arran, Paisley, 1919
Richard Sharpe Tr.	Adomnan of Iona, Life of Saint Columba, 1995
Ray Simpson	Celtic Spirituality, London, 1995
W.F.Skene	Celtic Scotland, 1886-1890
J.H.Smith	Constantine The Great, London 1971
P.Hately Waddell	Ossian, Glasgow, 1875
Martin Wallace	The Celtic Connection, 1995
W.J.Watson	History of the Celtic Place Names of Scotland, Dublin, 1986
G. Wright	Jura's Heritage, Jura, 1991
J.A.Balfour Ed.	The Book of Arran, Archaeology, 1910
W.M.Mackenzie Ed.	The Book of Arran, History and Folklore, Glasgow, 1914